D0379098

Other books in the Perfect Phrases series include:

Perfect Phrases for Performance Reviews by Douglas Max and Robert Bacal

Perfect Phrases for Setting Performance Goals by Douglas Max and Robert Bacal

Perfect Phrases for Customer Service by Robert Bacal

Perfect Phrases for the Perfect Interview by Carole Martin

Perfect Phrases for Managers and Supervisors by Meryl Runion

Perfect Phrases for Resumes by Michael Betrus

Perfect Phrases for Documenting Employee Performance Problems by Anne Bruce

Perfect Phrases for Cover Letters by Michael Betrus

Perfect Phrases for Motivating and Rewarding Employees by Harriet Diamond and Linda Diamond

Perfect Phrases for Business Letters by Ken O'Quinn

Perfect Phrases for Business Proposals and Business Plans by Don Debelak

Perfect Phrases for the Sales Call by Bill Brooks

Perfect Phrases for Executive Presentations by Alan M. Perlman

Perfect Phrases for Negotiating Salary and Job Offers

Perfect Phrases for Negotiating Salary and Job Offers

Hundreds of Ready-To-Use Phrases to Help You Get the Best Possible Salary, Perks, or Promotion

Matthew J. DeLuca and Nanette F. DeLuca

McGraw-Hill
New York Chicago San Francisco Lisbon
London Madrid Mexico City Milan New Delhi
San Juan Seoul Singapore Sydney Toronto

1 2 3 4 5 6 7 8 9 0   FGR/FGR   0 9 8 7 6

ISBN-13: 978-0-07-147551-8
ISBN-10: 0-07-147551-6

McGraw-Hill books are available at special quantity discounts to use as premiums and sales promotions, or for use in corporate training programs. For more information, please write to the Director of Special Sales, Professional Publishing, McGraw-Hill, Two Penn Plaza, New York, NY 10121-2298. Or contact your local bookstore.

Library of Congress Cataloging-in-Publication Data

DeLuca, Matthew J.
  Perfect phrases for negotiating salary and job offers : hundreds of ready-to-use phrases to help you get the best possible salary, perks, or promotion / Matthew J. DeLuca and Nanette F. DeLuca.
     p. cm.
  ISBN 0-07-147551-6 (alk. paper)
  1. Employment interviewing. 2. Job offers 3. Salaries. 4. Employee fringe benefits. 5. Promotions. 6. Negotiation in business—Terminology. I. DeLuca, Nanette F. II. Title. III. Title: Negotiating salary and job offers.

HF5549.5.I6D454 2007

650.14—dc22   2006031080

Contents

Part One: Preparing for Salary Negotiation — 1

Where Are You Coming From? What Is Your Current Situation? — 4
  Out of Work — 4
  You Are Currently Employed — 5
  You Are in the Middle of a Job Hunt — 7

Why Do You Think You Should Get Paid More Money?
  Why Now? — 8
  Emotions versus Pragmatics — 8
  What Is Your Role in the Company as Opposed to
    Your Stated Position? — 9

How to Create and Expand Your Knowledge Base — 10
  What You Need to Know—and Why — 10
  Research Your Selling Points — 11
  Research the Current Job Market, Industry, and Economy — 13
  Research Your Options — 15
  Thinking Outside of the Pay Envelope — 16

Define Compensation: What Does It Mean to You? — 17

What Are the Costs of the New Job? — 17

Looking the Part — 17

Transportation — 18

Contents

Make a Plan   19
  Crunching Numbers   19
  Negotiation Framework   23

Reconsider Your Bargaining Points   26
  *First Rule of Negotiation: Do Not Negotiate If You
    Do Not Want the Job*   26
  *Second Rule of Negotiation: Be Careful about
    What You Ask For*   27

How to Negotiate   28
  How Do You Negotiate?   28
  How Should *You Negotiate?*   28
  With Whom Should You Negotiate?   30
  When Should You Talk Money?   30
  Should Your Future Be Held Hostage to Your Past?   31

Rules—You Need to Know Them before
  You Can Break Them   32

Negotiating Guidelines   32
  Examining the Offer(s)   33
  Closing the Negotiations   34

Electronic versus Hardcopy Applications   34
  Online Applications   34
  Hardcopy Applications   35

Recruiters and Headhunters: Are They Useful in the
  Negotiating Process?   36

Part Two: Dealing with Salary Questions before and during the Recruiting and Selection Process   39

Opportunities That Require a Written Response   41

Questions That May Arise at Courtesy Interviews and
  Information-Gathering Sessions   44

Contents

Salary Questions That May Arise at Any Time   47

Submitting a Salary Number versus a Salary Range   50

Responding to Objections Raised by Headhunters, Human
Resources Professionals, or Hiring Managers   53

Responding to Objections If You Are a Job Seeker
Fifty Years Old or Older   57

Part Three: How to Negotiate the Total Compensation Offer: Salary, Benefits, and Perquisites   59

Responding to an Initial Offer   61
Asking for a Job Offer in Writing   64
If Written Job Offers Are Not Provided   64

Negotiating a Higher Salary   65

Negotiating a Sign-on Bonus   66

Negotiating a Bonus   67

Negotiating Options   68

Negotiating a Shorter Review Period   70

Negotiating a Different Starting Date   72

Negotiating Pay for COBRA Coverage   73

Negotiating the Ability to Work from Home   74

Negotiating Flexible Hours   74

Negotiating a Four-Day Week   76

Negotiating for a Laptop Computer, Cell Phone, and/
or Blackberry   77

Negotiating Authorization to Attend Professional Gatherings
Such as Conferences, Seminars, and Workshops   78

Negotiating Reimbursement for Professional Association
Memberships, Certifications, or Journals   79

Contents

Asking for a Contract   80

Securing the Promise of Severance   81

Negotiating Tuition Refund   83

Negotiating Child Care   85

Negotiating Benefits   86

Negotiating Additional Vacation Time / Time Off   88
  Vacation   88
  Sabbaticals   90
  Time Off for Religious Activities   90

Counteroffers   90
  *Type A: A Second Level of Negotiation with Your
      Would-Be New Employer*   90
  Type B: Negotiation with Your Current Employer   91

Dealing with Multiple Job Offers   93

Finalizing the Offer   94
  Accepting the Offer   95
  Declining the Offer   96
  If You Do Not Get a Job Offer   97

Part Four: Negotiating at Your Current Job   99

Performance Reviews   101
  Phrases for Discussing Performance   101
  Phrases for Salary Review   103
  If the Increase Is Unacceptable to You   105

How to Ask for a Raise or Promotion   107
  At the Completion of a Project   107
  Because of Market Conditions   108
  Because of Personal Issues   110
  Because of Internal Inequity   112
  If You Have Received Another Offer   114
  *If You Suspect Another Person Has Been Hired to
      Replace You*   117

Contents

Asking for a Promotion   119

Following a Compliment for Good Work   119

*If the Person Leaves Who Was Occupying a Position
That You Want*   119

If Your Supervisor Is Leaving   120

When a New Supervisor Arrives   121

If You Just Think It's Time   122

If You're No Longer Feeling Challenged   123

*As an Act of Desperation When There's No Money
for an Increase*   124

Phrases for Terminations, Downsizing, or Quitting   126

Phrases for Quitting That Leave the Door Open   126

Phrases for Being Downsized or Terminated   126

Phrases for Severance Negotiation   127

For an Overview Discussion   127

Severance Pay   128

Setting a Departure Date   128

Asking for a Letter of Reference   130

Staying on as a Consultant   130

Outplacement Assistance   131

Benefit Coverage (or Extended COBRA Coverage)   132

Active Employee Health Insurance Coverage   133

Pension Retirement Vesting   134

Tuition Refund Payments   134

E-Mail Access   135

Retention of Office Equipment and Services   136

*Continued Voice Mail for an Extended Period
(For Example, Six Months)*   136

Copying Personal Files   137

*If Asked to Sign Additional Agreements [For Example,
Noncompete, Nondisclosure (Confidentiality),
and No Solicitation]*   137

Contents

Part Five: Perfect Phrases for Special Circumstances   139

If You Have Been Working Per Diem   141

If You Have Been Working on Project-Based Freelance Independent
Contractor Assignments   142

Special Phrases for Sales Professionals (or Others with
Salary Plus Commissions)   144

Special Phrases for Wait Staff (or Any Other Position Where Most of
Your Earnings Come in Tips)   144

Being Paid "Off the Books" or Being "Grossed Up"   145

Phrases to Use If a Past Employer Invites You Back   147

Appendix A: Determining Your Current Level of Compensation and "Total Pay" Package   149

Understanding How Compensation Works   151
The Criteria for Some Salary Increases   152
How to Determine Your "Total Pay" Package   153
Determining Hourly Rates of Pay or Annual Salary   153
Thinking in Terms of Total Compensation   154
What Is Included in Compensation?   154

Appendix B: Sample Letters for Wrapping Up Negotiations   159

Offer Letter   161

Thank-You and Acceptance Letter   163

Confirmation Letter (If the Job Offer Is Not Given in Writing)   164

Contents

Declination and Thank-You Letter   166

Thank-You Letter (No Job Offer Received)   167

Authors' Answer Key   168

Appendix C: Resources   169

Web Sites   171

Suggested Readings   172

Perfect Phrases for Negotiating Salary and Job Offers

Part One

Preparing for Salary Negotiation

Money is an uncomfortable topic for most employees as well as for employers and interviewers. Many people have no idea what their parents, their friends, or even their spouse "really" makes. Certainly, no one can easily ask a coworker or friend, "How much is your annual salary?" So, we head into an interview situation with little or no practice talking about the subject of money. Maybe we enter with a lot of personal baggage, too. Add to this the lack of practice in interviewing and, most importantly, listening, and the whole conversation can be totally frustrating.

Even if you are not considering looking for a new job or are not in the middle of a job search, you will probably face discussions about your salary at annual reviews or when considering promotions or transfers. Few employees plan ahead for these important discussions; as a result they may act out of stress, embarrassment, or unease when the subject is broached.

A good manager makes plans for these discussions, and certainly an interviewer should be prepared for this integral part of the interview process, but in general many are not skilled in this regard. The most they might do is read off the salary level indicated on the job order they are seeking to fill. They are not equipped or empowered to negotiate a compensation package. The best tack to take when planning to talk about your compensation is to be prepared yourself. This preparation starts with some basic knowledge about yourself and your current situation.

Where Are You Coming From? What Is Your Current Situation?

Your outlook and your viewpoint are directly related to where you are standing right now and have a direct bearing on your negotiation dialogue. Are you currently employed and hoping for a raise? Jockeying for a better-paid position in the same company? Looking for a new job in a new company, doing the same type of work? Starting off on a new career path? Most of us will find ourselves in each of these situations, perhaps many times, during our working career. The following paragraphs discuss some of the common situations; each requires a different mode of operation.

Out of Work

There are diverse reasons why you may be unemployed at the current time, ranging from being downsized or quitting to raise a family or to go to school, to being fired for very apparent reasons (such as poor attendance or performance). You may see the handwriting on the wall and know it is a matter of time before your own position is eliminated in a management shake-up or divisional realignment. In each case, you need to do some basic preparation for your job search and inevitable money discussion.

If You Are Planning to Return to the Work Force
The duration and reason for your unemployment are pivotal to turning this into a positive element during the job interview. If you have been in the military, raising a family, or continuing your education, these are very common reasons for being out of work. Reevaluating your career path, travel, or other personal

reasons (caring for an ill relative or friend) are also explanations that the interviewer has probably heard before. It is not so much why you chose the path you have been on, or how long you have been on it, but what you have done to grow and remain current with your chosen industry or trade in the interim that is of more concern. The answer you give could very likely turn you into a valuable commodity.

If Your Job Search Has Been Unsuccessful and You Have Been Actively Searching for a Long Time

This is where you must be brutally honest: Are you qualified for the jobs you seek *and* for the compensation you are asking for? It may be time to retrench and reconsider job opportunities, at least for the short term. It may not be so much what you want to do but rather what you can do and what is available.

You are Currently Employed

Just because you have a good job in a company for which you enjoy working does not mean you are totally satisfied. It is human nature to always want more and better, and we define each of those terms uniquely. Below are some of the most common reasons for looking for a job while you are currently employed:

- **You are about to be fired.** Termination can be a strong reaction to many situations in the workplace. Did you step on the wrong toes? Did your performance not meet expectations? Having a good sense of why you are being or might be terminated is important. More to the point, what will your former employer say about you, your performance, and the reasons you are no longer employed there? (Many employers, to avoid legal issues, merely confirm dates of employment, but it can be a small world; "unofficial" information can be leaked, to your detriment.) Falsifying information on a job application or in an interview can be grounds for dismissal. And, of course, the question "why did you leave your last job?" will come up in an interview.

- **You are about to be downsized.** Are you being offered a severance package? Offered "early retirement"? Is there any outplacement assistance being offered? Sometimes there is opportunity for negotiation. Examples include: lump-sum payouts, annuity-type payment packages, health-care coverage, pension and/or retirement benefits.
- **You are ready to quit.** If you can stay, don't quit! Look at the situation in the most practical terms, including monetary issues. You may feel it would not be worth losing your sanity to stay, but then again, can't you take a deep breath and give it some time while you intensify your job search? You are more marketable as a current employee than as an unemployed one. Additionally, the reasons you cite for quitting will impact on your future employment and compensation.
- **You are seeking more pay for the same job.** You like what you are doing and want to keep on doing it, but you would like to be paid better. Why? Is there a market demand for your expertise that the company does not recognize? Can you earn more if you go elsewhere? Have you gained insight and experience that is not being reflected in your pay statement? Over the years, has your job changed—increased in scope and responsibilities—

while your salary has not kept pace? (Often, with the downsizing in recent years in many industries, the employees that are retained find themselves doing extra work to cover the growing workload without any compensatory increase in pay.)

- **You are looking to make a lateral move.** With internal job postings, you may have your eyes on a similar job in a different location or different division. Some interviews will be in order, and you may want to review your compensation package in light of changes in commute, cost of living in new area, or relocation expenses.

- **It is time for your annual performance review.** How would you rate your performance to date? How do you think your supervisor-manager will rate you? Do you have facts and figures to illustrate the value you have added and the contributions you have made over the past employment period? Has your employer codified merit increases? Are there caps on total increases per department or division?

- **You are seeking a promotion.** You have been on a path to a career change, perhaps taking classes, joining professional organizations, or just learning on the job. There is a job opening in the organization for which you feel you are the ideal candidate. You may be competing with external candidates, so you must be accurate in assessing your skill and expertise as well as your market value.

You Are in the Middle of a Job Hunt

You have been sending out targeted cover letters and résumés, going on interviews, and are actively seeking employment.

Since you are preparing to make a career move, you should have looked into market demand and pay for your level of skill and experience. You have an idea of the pay range for the particular position for which you are interviewing. You are likely to be faced with any of the following situations when you are looking for a job.

- **You are looking for a similar job in a new company or industry.** Your key selling points are "been there, done that . . . and can do it better for you than anyone else."
- **You are looking for a different job in a different company.** You have to identify and sell comparative skills and experiences, reinventing your career on the way. You might have to take a pay cut to reestablish yourself in a new career path.
- **You have gotten a counteroffer.** You have interviewed outside the company, received a job offer and have planned to accept it. When you inform your current employer of your plans, a counteroffer to retain you is made. Now what? Do you consider it? Are you a "suspect" employee, since you thought to leave? Are you leaving the devil you know for the devil you don't know? How firm is the offer? What is the counteroffer?

Why Do You Think You Should Get Paid More Money? Why Now?

Emotions versus Pragmatics

Your employer does not care about your finances. He or she is not interested in what the condition of your car is, how many mouths you have to feed, or when your mother-in-law is coming to live with you and what you need to do to renovate your home to accommodate her.

Employers may be family oriented and have day-care facilities and excellent family leave benefits, but the bottom line is, what value do you have to offer to the company? You either increase the revenue stream or help to reduce expenses. You need to quantify your value. For example, "I add 7 percent in sales,""I have cut expenses $10,000,""My department increased production 12 percent."The magic number for each employee is a number that reflects your worth to the employer, what you need to earn, and how you want to be compensated.

What Is Your Role in the Company as Opposed to Your Stated Position?

We have all known people in organizations that may have a lower job title but who may literally run the office. Their actual value added in the organization is not consistent with their job title or position. Sometimes, sadly, the opposite may be true: some folks are promoted over their abilities and reflect it in their job performance.

If you are going to make a case for yourself that leads to increased compensation, you need to examine what you actually do versus what your job title is. Perhaps your position needs to be reevaluated or a new job description created to reflect the current status. For example, an accountant position may only be slated for a salary range in the mid-five figures but an accountant-auditor may command additional salary. Do not assume that the Powers That Be know or understand what your job is or what the extent of your contribution has been. Be prepared with talking points of goals achieved or exceeded, additional responsibilities assumed, or projects completed.

How to Create and Expand Your Knowledge Base

What You Need to Know—and Why

As already mentioned, you cannot assume that supervisors know and understand exactly what it is that you do, or the extent of the value you add to the organization. Or, more importantly, you can't be sure that they have included this information in any memos or recommendations regarding salary increases or promotions. It cannot hurt to sell your accomplishments and experiences again.

You especially need to sell your accomplishments when you apply for a job outside of your current organization. Why? Because similarly named positions in one company may carry completely different responsibilities in another. For example, a receptionist for Company A may just be required to greet arrivals, while a receptionist at Company B may have to handle telephones, schedule meetings and conference room usage, and deal with many different foreign visitors while doing light word processing. You need to be able to relate job requirements in the job to which you are applying to your skill set, experience, and compensation in the previous (or current) one. Crucial, too, is the need to understand the requirements of the potential new job, because you cannot sell yourself until you have an understanding of what your potential employer needs; what they are buying.

Research Your Selling Points

Skills Inventory and Work Experience

Periodically, you ought to take an inventory of your skills. Use the following worksheet to list skills such as excellent time management, familiarity with computer programs, management experience, and language proficiencies. State where and when each skill was used, and provide an example of how the skill relates to your current position or the position being sought.

Skills Inventory Worksheet		
Skills	**Where/When Used**	**Example**

The same is true for your work experiences. Starting with your most recent job, list your work history. Include dates of employment and key skills and responsibilities. Also note both what your entry level was and what your title and responsibilities were when you left.

Skills Inventory Worksheet		
Employer's Name Address	**Dates Employed (from ___ to___) Reason for Leaving**	**Key Responsibilities, Achievements, Skills**
1		
2		
3		
4		
5		

Research the Current Job Market, Industry, and Economy

With the availability of the Internet, accessed either through your own home computer or public terminals at neighborhood libraries, Internet cafés, and other locations, there is little excuse for being uninformed. Additionally, many occupations require or appreciate computer skills and the ability to be a savvy Internet user. Check out some of the following locations in cyberspace.

- **Employer's Web site.** You can get a wide range of information from your company's Web site, including current job postings, press releases, and insight into their current operations.

- **Other employers' Web sites.** Corporate Web sites of companies in the industry other than the one to which you are applying, which have jobs similar to the one you are seeking, in the same locale, can also provide information relative to current salaries being offered as well as general information about the industry itself.

- **Industry and professional Web sites.** Major industries and professions, for example information technologies, librarians, and accountants, maintain Web sites with information specific to their interests.

- **Local/city Web sites.** Some local and regional Web sites offer job boards and corporate information on major employers in the area.

- **Sites for general salary information.** These include Abbott, Langer & Associates, www.abbott-langer.com CareerJournal.com, www.careerjournal.com

Salary.com, www.salary.com
SalaryExpert.com, www.salaryexpert.com
U.S. Department of Labor, www.bls.gov/ncs/ocs/
compub.htm (for free pay surveys)

At the Library

The following information services are available at most public libraries: ABI Global, Business Source Premier, LexisNexis, and ProQuest Newsstand. So is JobStart (jobstar.org/tools/salary/index.php).

Job Posting Sites

Many of the sites offering free résumé posting services also offer insight into the going rate for specific jobs posted by employers. You can get information relating to skills and experience requirements as they relate to the salary levels cited. Visit some of the following sites:

- EmploymentGuide.com (www.employmentguide.com; (go to "Career Resources")
- Monster.com (www.monster.com; go to "Career Advice")
- USAJOBS (www.usajobs.opm.gov, for jobs in the government sector)

You can also use a search engine such as Google.com to search for "salary," "job openings," or the job you are seeking to find more specific information.

Classified Ads

Even if you are not seeking a new job, ads in local newspapers or circulars can provide information on what local employers are offering for similar positions.

Research Your Options

Sometimes you cannot evaluate an offer unless you know what your alternatives are. What if your current employer does not give you a higher salary? What if you cannot find a job with the compensation that you need at this time? Suppose you can't find a job with the compensation you need in the industry in which you are looking. What if you can't find a job in the geographic location you prefer? Understanding what choices you have available to you will help you to determine what actions you can take and the inherent costs of decisions made or postponed.

Relocate

You might want to or have to consider the option of relocating to a different area because of economic conditions, a lack of opportunities, or loss of alternative employers in your job area. Cost of living may be lower in another city, which may alter your compensation requirements. Other cities may have a greater demand for your line of work or expertise.

Change Employer, Industry, or Job

Technology may be making your skills obsolete. The industry where you are seeking employment may be stagnant and in a downturn. Perhaps you need to rethink your career as a whole. If you cannot seem to find employment at compensation levels that you seek, you may need to upgrade your skills. You may have to consider other areas that can use your existing skills—many are transferable—in another career path.

Stay Exactly Where You Are

If a salary increase is not offered at this time and there do not seem to be alternative employers with job offers that are commensurate with your compensation goals, this may be the handwriting on the wall telling you to bide your time and stay where you are. You can ask that you be considered for an increase, promotion, or transfer in the future, should the situation change; or negotiate some alternatives to a bigger paycheck.

Quit

If the job is intolerable and the circumstances are such that getting no salary is better than enduring this situation, you may feel that there is no alternative but to tender your resignation. Think twice. A question often asked in interviews is why you left your most recent job, and once you have resigned, the sudden departure will have to be explained (often repeatedly) when you seek other employment. It is far better to stay employed while you seek another job. Or ask your current employer for a compromise: request to revisit the situation in three months, or six months. Determine if improvement on your part will paint a more favorable picture. Alternatively, being able to devote all of your time and energies to seeking a new position may be the best choice for you at this time.

Thinking Outside of the Pay Envelope

What you earn is not always included in your direct deposit statement. Compensation is made up of many elements other than salary alone. You need to think in terms of total compensation—a package of payments and benefits, tangible and intangible—when you think of what you should be paid.

Define Compensation: What Does It Mean to You?

In the scenarios described earlier, each employee in each of those positions might have a totally different definition of "salary." One may really need the cash flow now to meet current debts or personal obligations. Another may discount any retirement benefits because of his or her young age. Yet another employee may be willing to trade off salary for a comprehensive health-care package or a less time-consuming commute. An accurate assessment of "must haves," "nice to haves," and "giveaways" will form the basis for compensation negotiation. For a more in-depth discussion of what constitutes compensation and how you can measure your total compensation, see Appendix A.

What Are the Costs of the New Job?

It is not enough to consider all that you might get with a new position, you must also consider real and intangible costs.

Looking the Part

In every job from fast food to graphic design to accountant, there is a certain expected standard of appearance. For some, this may necessitate extensive purchasing of clothing. A recent college graduate may not have the professional wardrobe needed for corporate offices, for example. Someone transferring from a large city might be overdressed for a business-casual environment in another town. These costs must be evaluated as "start-up expenses."

Transportation

How will you get to your new job? Public transportation? Driving? Do you have a car—a car that can make the daily trip? What will be the cost of commuting: tolls, gas, parking, and repairs on the car?

Commuting Time

What is the daily time commitment? Just because you do not get paid from the time you go out your door does not mean you should not consider it an inherent cost of doing business. If you are going from a 15-minute walk to a local job to a 90-minute morning commute in rush hour, this will have an impact on your life.

Lifestyle Impact

Each business fosters its unique environment and places its stamp on the workplace. Are there cubicles or private offices, or one large room with many desks? How private a person are you? Do you need to decorate your personal space with pictures, mementos of your private life? Look around—is this the norm? Conversely, if you feel strongly that home and work lives are totally separate, will an environment with many family-oriented activities be a blessing or a curse? While specifics of religion, politics, and sexual orientation are not to be considered in the hiring process nor in deciding future compensation/salary increases/promotions (as per Title VII of the Civil Rights Act, as amended), they can be a large factor in the corporate culture. You can feel comfortable, productive, and valued—or you cannot.

Other Commitments

Are you involved in other activities? Family obligations? Taking classes or teaching? How will they be affected? For example, you may need to leave early one day a week to continue a class that is already in progress; this can be a point of salary negotiation.

Make a Plan

You need to have a clear idea of what is important to you in any job: the new one you are considering or perhaps the next one that comes your way. This is your plan for now; in a year or two it may be completely different as circumstances and your life change.

Crunching Numbers

Before getting involved in any negotiation, use the following worksheet to develop your own salary history. Try to remember starting salaries, promotions and increases, and ending salaries for prior and current jobs. Also indicate what benefits you received (various elements may include: bonus, profit sharing, medical insurance, child-care facilities, and transportation subsidies).

Salary History Worksheet		
Employer	**Starting Salary and Position Ending Salary and Position**	**Benefits**
1		
2		
3		
4		
5		

Second, have a firm idea of what you really need in terms of cash flow. Use the following worksheet to outline your expenses. List your fixed monthly expenses such as rent/mortgage, utilities, insurances (home, life, auto), groceries, and transportation. Then add on discretionary spending needs (for example, entertainment, travel). Blank spaces are provided for additional expenses such as alimony, child care.

Expenses Worksheet		
Housing Expenses		**Monthly Estimates**
	Rent/Maintenance	$
	Mortgage	$
	Utilities	$
	Repairs/Upkeep	$
	Telephone/Internet/Cable	$
Insurance	Life, Auto, Homeowners	$
Debt Coverage	Loans, Credit Cards	$

Living Expenses	Groceries	$
	Clothing	$
	Medical, Dental	$
	Transportation	$
Work Related		
	Education	$
	Memberships, Subscriptions	$
	Transportation	$
Discretionary Spending		
	Entertainment	$
	Travel	$
	Total Monthly	$
	× 12 for Annual Expenses	$

Expenses Worksheet

Last, you need to do some research into what range of salary can be anticipated. If the average salary paid is in the high five figures, it would be foolish to ask for only $50,000! Know your competition and what the job itself is worth—and what your experience and skill level can command.

Negotiation Framework

Look at the Compensation Package Worksheet that follows. Consider this a shopping list for negotiating your compensation package. List everything you can think of that you want on the next worksheet. Then consider what you really need and what would be the icing on the cake. Certain levels of cash flow are required to support the annual expenses you listed in the Expenses Worksheet. In addition, other compensation elements such as benefits, bonuses, and health care must be considered on an annual basis. Establish ranges for these negotiation points.

Compensation Package Worksheet		
	I need	**I want**
Cash Flow		
Salary (Take-Home Pay)	$	$
Annual Bonus	$	$
Profit Sharing	$	$
Review Period	___ Months	___ Months
Benefits		
Health Care		
Vacation		
Child Care		
Transportation		

Preparing for Salary Negotiation

Perks		
Title		
Office		
Expense Account		
Company Car		
Intangibles		
Work Schedule (Hours)		
Commutation (Time)		
Location/Environment		
Corporate Culture		

Must Haves

These must-have items are not negotiable. If the single most important aspect to you is a required amount of take-home pay, then that element is not negotiable and will not be affected by a counteroffer of a corner office or other perks. Conversely, if you do not need child-care facilities, that benefit will not interest you.

Nice to Haves

The nice to haves are those "well, if they are offering it . . ." kinds of things. These would make your life nice and easier, but they are not absolutely necessary.

Giveaways

These are things the company will probably offer but that don't mean that much to you. You can control disclosure of these facts. If you don't need or want some perks, possibly you can offer them back to the company in exchange for some must haves.

Reconsider Your Bargaining Points

You have this all down on paper—now to get ready to put it into action.

First Rule of Negotiation: Do Not Negotiate If You Do Not Want the Job

Sometimes the hardest thing to do is to walk away. If you need to walk away, thank them very sincerely for their time and consideration in making the job offer and explain that, after careful deliberation, you do not feel this is the right move for you to make at this time.

If Only the Job Was ...

Sometimes it is not the money but other aspects of the job that need to be negotiated. The starting date does not work for you—there is a serious conflict with family plans. Or, the commute would be immensely easier if you could come in a half-hour earlier and then leave earlier. Don't confuse these issues with salary.

Know Your Ranges

As you move along your job search or in your career, you may change your demands in reaction to market conditions. Maybe it is not so much of a seller's market, as you had thought. You really need to have a range in mind of what the minimum you would accept to take the job or make the move. Sometimes you have to think long-range and consider the current, prospective move to be a step in the right direction and not the end goal.

Second Rule of Negotiation: Be Careful About What You Ask For

Look at your list of must haves. Are you going to be comfortable asking for all that? Be sure that you are at ease with staking your job offer on these points. If you feel comfortable that you have considered all facets rationally, not emotionally, then you are ready to learn how to negotiate.

Remember to be careful what you ask for. For example, if you ask for a better review period and they comply with your request, you are now put in the position of having to accept the job because they ostensibly removed the one obstacle you raised. If you state that you feel the position, considering your experience, should pay a few thousand dollars more and then they come back to you and meet your offer with a sign-on bonus, you may have painted yourself into a corner.

How to Negotiate

Negotiating from strength is always preferred but not always possible. This preparation should help you to think on your feet. Planning and anticipation is essential when you are the one initiating the conversation about your salary, such as when you are asking for a promotion or transfer, or when you are seeking to renegotiate your whole compensation package. Annual reviews and employment interviews are key times to prepare yourself in advance.

How Do You Negotiate?

Have you successfully negotiated in the past? Did you purchase a car, a house? What about past jobs? What do you remember about your experiences? Did you even think in terms of negotiation, or were you just so excited to get the job offer that you snapped it up? Or, did you ever negotiate yourself out of a job? What would you do over if you could? What do you think your weakest areas were?

How *Should* You Negotiate?

Many people try the oblique approach to avoid directly asking their boss for a salary increase: they discuss it with their colleagues and hope their boss hears about their interest, or they drop hints to test the waters ("Gee, I heard that Joe in the other division got a big increase; business must be good"). Others go to their boss, hat in hand, explaining their situation ("Putting two kids through college is expensive"); some go over their boss's head, and a few even demand an increase while threatening to quit if they are not accommodated. These are all emotional tactics, not professional, planned negotiations.

Salaries are affected by many factors: market forces (the cost of replacing the employee), the contribution that the employee makes, geographic conditions (economy, supply and demand for services), as well as the profitability of the organization itself. A growing company, stretching its finances, is a different entity than a mature, stable, profitable company.

Look the Part
Aside from surprise situations at work, such as being summoned into your boss's office to be told you are being downsized to a lower salary, you should dress the part for any scheduled negotiation sessions. Look professional and confident. As in all other interview situations, be aware of body language. Sit up, make eye contact, don't fidget or slouch.

Listen to What Is Being Said
Listen to what is said—by you, by them. Most of us learn to read and write, but seldom are we taught to listen. We are usually planning what we are going to say next, rather than hearing what the other person is saying.

Let Them Talk

When you are very eager to make your own comments, it is often difficult not to interrupt. Don't; that's frequently a problem in interviews. Let the other person finish speaking. When you cut someone off midsentence, you may have assumed incorrectly what they were going to say, and you are being impolite. So, slow it down. Be an active listener. Eye contact, head nods, and facial expressions all show that you are with them as they speak.

With Whom Should You Negotiate?

You should be talking with the decision maker. Who, exactly, will make the job offer? It may be the division or district head, the human resources manager, or senior management. If the person with whom you are talking has to take the offer or counteroffer to someone else for approval (for example, if you are dealing with a recruiter who needs to get back to the employer), then that adds another element of time and risk in the negotiation. If possible, ask, "Who will be making the final decision? Perhaps I should be speaking with him or her directly?"

When Should You Talk Money?

During a job search, you expect that the topic of pay will come up. In fact, you want it to—you need to know how much they will pay you. Salary requirements can be requested on a job application, a form to be submitted when you e-mail your résumé to a job search database, or in your initial interview. Ideally, salary should be part of the negotiations *after* you have received a job offer. But often interviewers use salary as a screening technique. The trick is not to be screened out (unless, of course, the salary levels are totally unacceptable, no matter how many perks are added). This is where your research into expected salary levels pays off.

Should Your Future Be Held Hostage to Your Past?

Your salary history can be a sticking point for some interviewers. There can be a feeling that you should not make a big change—either up or down. The best attitude for you to radiate is "that was then, this is now—and this is here." It is a new job in a new organization or division, and the past should not predict the present. Even though you may have tried to sell the fact that your experiences are similar to those in the new job, also be ready to point out (if you are asking for a higher salary) extra responsibilities and new skills being used. The fact that your expenses or needs are higher may not be a huge reason for an employer to offer more, but if that is the deal breaker, discuss it. For example, if there is a waiting period for health benefits and this will cause you to have to go on COBRA (for more on COBRA, see Part Three, "Negotiating Pay for COBRA Coverage"), the employer may not increase your base salary but may offer a sign-on bonus to cover your health-care out-of-pocket costs until you are fully covered under their plan.

Stay in the Game

Don't get screened out if you are asked about salary early in the interview process, before a job offer is on the horizon. Talk in terms of salary ranges and total compensation packages. If you have done your research, you should not be out of the ballpark with your figures. Do not be afraid to ask, "How much are you willing to pay for this position?" Get to a negotiation point, not a flat turn-down. Show that you are flexible, if indeed you are. This is where the three worksheets in this chapter come in handy. If the starting salary offered is low, for example, perhaps they will agree to a salary review in three or six months instead of an annual review. The main thing is to keep the conversation going and remain flexible.

Rules—You Need to Know Them before You Can Break Them

Employers have budgets, salary levels, benchmarks. Despite the fact that you are an excellent candidate, a valued employee, and a bargain at any price, sometimes employers cannot meet your compensation requirements because of internal restrictions. For example, perhaps the company is at the end of its budget period and has simply run out of funds, budgetwise, for hiring more staff. Or they could be long overdue for updating their job descriptions and salary levels to keep up with the marketplace. These are considerations on which you cannot have an impact—other than asking to be kept in mind when the situation changes.

Negotiating Guidelines

With all the research and practice completed, and knowing that there really are no hard and fast rules, you should still keep in mind the following general points in every negotiation.

Silence can be a tool. When asked a question, answer and then be quiet. Do not say more than you need to.

Control disclosure. "Just the facts." It is tempting to tip your hand too early, letting them know for example that you are *really* interested in the position (almost at any price.

Be firm in what you say. "No" means "no". Use it wisely. Know what is absolutely nonnegotiable for you—and why.

Be consistent. Once agreement has been reached on any point, move on. Do not revisit it.

Remember what is important to you. Stay focused on a few central points. Don't get side-tracked and come home forgetting to ask a key question.

Find out when they need an answer. Do not be pressured to give an answer too soon; ask for time to think it over. When must the position be filled?

Ask for the offer, with all details, to be put in writing. Request that it be in e-mail, regular mail, fax—whatever.

Keep the door open. Even if you are unable to strike a deal this time, maintain cordial relations should another position become open later on. Put your appreciation in writing, with a thank-you note, to everybody with whom you deal.

Examining the Offer(s)

With written offer in hand, you need to make a decision. Break down the offer in terms of compensation and intangibles, and compare it to your current position and/or your "needs and wants" profile. If you have received a counteroffer or if you are comparing two different job offers, this exercise is important for you to do, so you can make an informed decision. This exercise can also be done when you are offered a severance package. Review the terms, and determine if they are sufficient for your needs.

Closing the Negotiations

If the terms are satisfactory, then the next question is, "When do I start?"

Should an impasse be reached where neither you nor the employer can find an agreeable solution, then it is important to leave on good terms. You never know when paths will cross again. If the situation changed, would you want to work here? If so, state as much in both a telephone conversation when you decline the job offer and in a follow-up letter thanking them for their time and offer of employment. Leave the door open. See Appendix B for sample letters you can use to wrap up the negotiation process.

Electronic versus Hardcopy Applications

Online Applications

The online job application is becoming more and more common. If you are completing an online application, be aware that electronic applications only accept numbers in a preset format, and that you will be unable to submit the application if fields are left blank.

Therefore, if you apply online, you must be prepared to submit something for a pay number (or numbers, if pay history is required). Keep in mind that your unwillingness to provide any number may lead to outright rejection of your application.

You will also see that pay information needs to be submitted in a certain way, so there will be no room to include "plus bonus," as in "$100,000 plus bonus." You will be allowed to enter numbers and usually decimals, but no words.

As with any salary discussion, when completing online applications you need to determine what your annual compensation will include.

Tips for Online Applications

- Be sure to keep a record of what pay information you submitted in your online application, along with a breakdown of your pay components, so that when the situation arises you are ready to negotiate with an accurate and complete recall of the information you already provided. Failure to do so puts the one holding the information at a major advantage, since they have your number (literally!) and you don't.
- Always try to remember to locate your application online before any contact with the prospective employer.
- When completing your online application, determine how easy it is to retrieve by trying to do so at that time.

Hardcopy Applications

Frequently, a hardcopy application includes a box that asks for desired salary. How do you get around it?

You don't. But be careful to disclose only what you need to, and remember to write down what number you submitted, as well as your thinking, so that you may recall them later. Consider the following responses:

- "Flexible"
- "Negotiable"
- "High 50s"

Recruiters and Headhunters: Are They Useful in the Negotiating Process?

When thinking about whether or not to use recruiters and headhunters, the key item you always need to keep in mind is the answer to the question, "Who are they working for?" To put it more bluntly, "Who pays them?" Always remember that recruiters are working for the client who is responsible for sending them their check, and it is the client, therefore, who gets to call all the shots.

Regardless of the type of recruiter you contact (there are two kinds, retainer and contingency), the goal of the recruiter is to make the client a happy client; the way to do that is to provide a successful hire who is being paid at the most cost-effective level. Retainer recruiters are sometimes referred to as "headhunters" because they are usually going after the biggest "game," that is, the highest-paid positions, and they get paid whether or not a successful placement is made. Contingency recruiters are paid only if they are responsible for introducing the successful hire to the client.

If the client says a number of skills are desirable, the recruiter will likely search for candidates who have only those skills. The same is true for compensation. Consider that the recruiter's payment is usually tied to the level of pay the successful candidate is offered. As a result, the higher the range of compensation to be offered, the better able the recruiter will be to get suitable candidates (from which pool the best candidate will be offered a job). This sounds like a perfect situation for you as a candidate—the more you are paid, the more the recruiter will earn. But keep in mind that the recruiter also wants to complete the placement as quickly and as effortlessly as possible.

Part Two

Dealing with Salary Questions before and during the Recruiting and Selection Process

The following are some common phrases you will see or hear when you are dealing with salary questions before and during the recruiting and selection process. Also shown are some effective responses to these comments.

Opportunities That Require a Written Response

Many opportunities require that responses be in writing, whether it be hardcopy applications, online applications, or responses to ads or job postings. In your written responses, you will frequently be asked for your desired salary and current salary. You can't get around it, but be careful to disclose only what you need to and remember to write down the details of the information you provide, as well as your thinking, so that you may recall them later. The following are some common phrases you will see or hear when you are applying for a job. Also shown are some desirable responses to these comments.

"Include your desired salary in your response."

- "Flexible"
- "Negotiable"
- "High 50s"
- "Low 70s"
- "$47,000.00"

- "I feel that a salary range of $50,000 to $60,000 would be consistent with both the current market for comparable jobs and my experience."
- "Considering current market conditions, the position as described in the posting, and both my experience and potential, I feel that a salary of $55,000 to $63,500 would be appropriate, but I would always consider the entire compensation package, including benefits."
- "I am looking for a pay level of $58,000 at this time and am flexible at that range."

"No résumés will be considered without current salary information."

- "I am currently earning $65,000."
- "I am currently earning $65,000 plus bonus. I would like to receive an amount of approximately 10 to 15 percent above that amount as an enticement to depart."
- "I am currently earning $65,000 plus an anticipated bonus of $3,000."
- "I am currently earning $65,000 and I am due for a raise next month."
- "I am currently earning $65,000 and I am anticipating a raise of $4,000 per year, effective next month."
- "In my current position, I am earning $65,000 plus bonus. I do not feel, however, that the pay my current employer provides fully compensates me for my current level of performance and the values I bring to the organization. I am hoping the position you describe seeks someone to perform at my level and will reward accordingly."

Dealing with Salary Questions before and during Recruiting

- "My most recent base pay is $48,000 per year."
- "With overtime, my annual pay will exceed $52,000 this year."
- "I anticipate that my most recent base pay with bonuses will be approximately $57,000 this year."
- "My current rate of pay, including shift premiums and bonus will reach $62,500 this year."
- "My most recent base pay, including an anticipated pay increase next month will reach the $65,000 level by year end."

"Please include your salary history in your response."

- "At my last three employers my pay ranged from $43,500 to $58,100."
- "While at my current organization, my pay has risen from $39,200 to $48,100, in the three years I have been there."
- "My pay history at my current employer is provided in this chart."

Salary Information Chart			
Sign-on Bonus		**$5,000.00**	
Date	**Event**	**Base/Increase Amount**	**Total Annualized Compensation**
3/23/2002	Offer of employment	$40,000.00	$40,000.00
12/31/2002	Review/merit increase	$2,500.00	$42,500.00
06/01/2003	Promotion increase	$4,500.00	$47,000.00
12/31/2003	Review/merit increase	$3,000.00	$50,000.00
12/31/2004	Review/merit increase	$5,000.00	$55,000.00
12/31/2005	Review/merit increase	$5,000.00	$55,000.00
Anticipated:			
9/30/2006	Promotion increase	$7,500.00	$62,500.00
12/31/2006	Review/merit increase	$5,500.00	$68,000.00

Questions That May Arise at Courtesy Interviews and Information-Gathering Sessions

Suppose, at an exploratory interview, you are faced with the following question.

"I am wondering whether you would be interested in discussing possible job openings while you are here? What salary are you looking for?"

Dealing with Salary Questions before and during Recruiting

What should your responses be? Here are some suggestions.

- "Let me say I am very interested in pursuing opportunities further while I am here today. While I appreciate your interest in discussing pay, I suggest that we should postpone any discussion of pay by saying that I am certain your organization, with the reputation it has, will pay appropriately if and when any job is offered."
- "Your offer catches me off guard. Let me discuss with Human Resources what your pay levels are and I am sure something can be worked out."

If you are speaking initially to HR:

- "Your offer catches me off guard. Let me postpone any discussion regarding pay at this time. I am very interested in working for this organization, and I am sure that at the right time we will arrive at a mutually acceptable pay rate for the job offered."
- "I am sure we will be able to come to an agreement about pay after you first decide that I am the right person for the job, so let me ask you to first make that decision. What else should we discuss at this time?"
- "To me there are more important matters than salary when we are discussing the job and what I can do for you. I am certain that, if I am the right person for the job, we will agree on a salary that works for us both. Tell me where you see the key to success in this job will be."
- "If we have a conversation now about salary, I am concerned that I will either be eliminated from consideration or locked in, so could we delay that

conversation until we discuss more about what you expect from this job?"
- "What do you currently pay for someone with my skills and experience?"

If the HR representative continues to pursue this line of questioning:

"I appreciate your flexibility, but I really want to see what your expectations are to ensure that we don't waste too much of your time before getting to that point."

- "Thanks and I appreciate that. My current salary is $57,500, and I assure you that to get the opportunity to join this organization, I would definitely consider a lateral move."
- "My current salary is $57,500, and I would hope that there would be some incentive provided when you invite me to join your organization."
- "My current salary is $57,500, and I also have a very generous benefits (and/or bonus incentive, and/or perks) program."
- "My current salary is $57,500, but it is a 24/7 situation and they pay accordingly."
- "In the organization where I am currently employed, I earn $38,000 annually. I don't know, though, how that translates to pay levels and jobs here."
- "From the research that I have done before today's visit, the range is $47,500 to $55,000. Is that your range for this position?"

- "I would really like to know more about your pay structure and benefits programs before discussing what I consider an appropriate base pay level. It would be helpful for me also to learn more about bonuses and performance review schedules before being able to really answer your question."

Salary Questions That May Arise at Any Time

"Would you consider a lateral move?"

- "To me the major issues are the company and the job. I want to work for an organization that is going to be around for quite a while. I would like to stay and become a part of what they do. If that means taking a pay cut in exchange for the security of knowing I will have a job every day, then that will be fine with me."
- "Perhaps to you it seems a lateral move, but to me it represents a real opportunity to finally get into the organization that I have been trying to join for quite a while. I am sure from what I know about this organization that once I prove myself the money will follow."
- "Absolutely. There are other factors to consider that go beyond monetary consideration."

"Would you consider a pay cut?"

- "Sorry, but with the personal obligations I currently have, it will be unreasonable to even think about doing so at this time."

- "In this market, one needs to be flexible. Let me know the specifics and I am sure we will be able to work out something that will be mutually acceptable."
- "We have talked about your concerns with my pay. I know you will not be able to pay me at the same level I was earning at my organization.[1] But I am hoping that we can discuss a flexible work arrangement that will allow me to offset that lower level of pay with a four-day workweek [or a work-at-home arrangement, reimbursement for gas and travel expenses, or meal money]."
- "While my primary concern is not money, I expect to be compensated fairly for the work I perform. Make me a fair offer based on your current situation and I am sure we will be able to work something out."
- "The opportunity you have described sounds like a great one to me. I would prefer to be paid by what I bring to the job, but I will be flexible on pay at this time."

"What is your current salary?"

- "My current pay is $50,000."
- "My current pay is $50,000, but I also receive a $15,000 bonus."
- "I appreciate your asking for my current rate of pay and not what I desire. I was hoping that you would be of some assistance here. I know that to get a person to accept a new job, a premium is usually provided as an enticement."

---

[1] Consider name dropping here to serve as a reminder for the prestigious organization you would be leaving, if, in fact, that is the case.

Dealing with Salary Questions before and during Recruiting

"What salary are you looking for?" Or "What salary range are you looking for?"

- "In my current job, I feel I am not being fairly rewarded and that has been okay, since I appreciate the fact that the organization was willing to train me and they took a gamble. Now, though, I have really demonstrated what I can do, but, my pay has not kept pace, for a variety of reasons. I really am looking to be paid what the market is paying for jobs such as mine."

- "I did some homework to prepare for today's interview, and I have found that a pay level of $38,000 to $45,000 for this job would be fair." [Make sure you feel confident with your research.]

- "I couldn't really say without a complete understanding of what I would be accountable for and without learning more about what your current compensation package includes. Can we talk more about it?"

- "Salary is certainly an important consideration, but I need to know more about your flexible work time and other benefits."

- "Please tell me more about what outcomes are expected from the position. Also, it would be helpful to know the functional and organizational title of the position to which this position reports. Last, please tell me what other positions report to the same incumbent."

- "My requirements are flexible. It is really the opportunity that is important to me at this time professionally."

- "Let me ask you, what is the range for this position?"

Then, if given a specific amount, ask as a follow-up question:

■ "Is that the midpoint of the range?" [Do not say the word *minimum*, nor do you want to suggest that it is the *maximum*.]

Then, if you do learn more details:

■ "Based on what you have told me about this position, a figure of $55,000 [or whatever the figure that would be okay *for you*] would be appropriate."

To address potential problems head on:

■ "I know that you may consider me overqualified for this position, but I need to be sure you are aware of extenuating circumstances that would make me an ideal candidate."
■ "I realize I am relocating from an area with high labor costs, so I was able to command a premium salary. I know that will not be the case here."
■ "I realize the for-profit sector has the resources to pay more. You know that the pay was not as high as it sounds, since for that pay I was on 24/7 call and probably logged a minimum of 50 hours a week."

Submitting a Salary Number versus a Salary Range

Whether you choose to submit one number or a range of numbers depends upon you. If you use one number, the risk is that the potential employer will say it is too high. (On rare occasions, you may be eliminated if you come in too low, so watch out for that risk also.) If you choose to mention a range instead, then you are indicating some willingness to be flexible with the pay level. Flexibility is good, but if they see that as an opportunity to give you a lower level of pay, then it is not so good! That said, we believe the best route is to provide a salary range, when possible. There are advantages in being flexible, especially when it comes time to negotiate (after the written offer is extended). For example:

- "When we first discussed pay levels of this position, I mentioned a range of $37,500 to $45,000. I used that number with confidence and based it on the level of understanding I had at that time that the rest of the pay package would be similar to the rest of my compensation arrangement at my current organization. After discussions with the benefits staff and reviewing the materials they provided, there are some major differences between what I will need to pay for here and my current employer. With that in mind I am hopeful that your base pay offer will be a higher one due to the additional out-of-pocket expenses I will have when [not *if*] I come here."
- "When we first met, my first priority was to see if there was a match for us. Now that we have moved along and I am really excited by what I see, I am also aware of some details that were not an issue back then.

The following are some examples of issues you could raise.

- "Where I currently work, I am very close to home. So, not only is the commute a short one, but I am able to get home for lunch on most days and easily arrive in time at day care to pick up my child. With this job opportunity—and I am really excited at the prospect of joining you—my commute time is suddenly an hour. So, not only is there going to be more wear and tear on the car, not to mention having to pay for more gasoline, for which prices are soaring, but additional expenses for lunch and new day-care arrangements. Now, I know all of these details are my concerns alone, but I hope that you would be understanding and do what you can to make the change a less difficult one by adding something to the base."

■ "I am not sure you are aware that, if I were to stay with my current employer, next month would be review time. Although I did not know it when we first met—in fact, I just learned it—I have been budgeted for a 15 percent increase and promotion. Now, you know what is really exciting to me is this opportunity; I am not coming here for the money. Still, I wonder if you might do something to the base to offset what I am leaving behind."

■ "I want to be sure you are aware that they just announced bonuses at my current employer. If I am there when the bonuses are distributed on July 30, I will be getting a check for $15,000. Is there anything that can be done to change the start date?" [Here, the key to remember is that you are not asking for more money, you are asking for a delay in your start date so you can collect the money due to you. Your new employer has to decide whether to let you stay where you are until the payout date so that you can collect your bonus, or whether they want you so badly that they're willing to pay you what you will miss.]

Negotiating salary offers will be covered in more detail in Part Three.

Responding to Objections Raised by Headhunters, Human Resources Professionals, or Hiring Managers

"I noticed that when you completed your application, you did not respond to the item asking for salary information."

- "The application asked for desired salary, and I just want you to know that I am flexible here. I also need to know more about what I will be doing here so that I am better able to gauge what your organization considers the value of the position."

- "My recruiter suggested that I leave all salary matters, including questions and requests for information, to her."

- "If you simply want me to provide the specific information regarding pay levels at my current and past employers, let me write in the missing information and I look forward to proceeding. However, I prefer not to engage in salary discussions until such a time as you decide to make me an offer."

- "Quite frankly, I did not want to eliminate myself from further consideration, so that was why I left it blank. I know that the position I am applying for here is different from what I have been doing. I will be flexible about the pay, since that is not my biggest concern. I would like to see if there is opportunity for me to quickly add value to you. I am sure at the appropriate time, if there is continued interest, we will be able to come to terms favorable to us both."

■ "The recruiter [or the person doing the screening or any prior interview] described your organization, and she mentioned it was very competitive. She also told me that, to stay that way, you always strive to hire top talent. With those comments, I am confident that, if and when an offer is made, it will be both attractive and fair."

"Your desired salary is a little rich. What you are asking for may be more than the company [or client] is willing or able to pay. Do you have any flexibility in what it may take for you to consider this or another opportunity?"

■ "I am very willing to be flexible; however, I also have done my research before today's meeting and I feel that my current rate of pay is actually slightly below what the going rate is. Do you agree?"

■ "Sorry, but I don't feel I should consider a move without some cash incentives to offset the risk that goes with a new job."

■ "This sounds like a great opportunity, but please also keep in mind that the commute is a much longer one. I am certainly willing to accept a longer trip for the right opportunity; however, I am also interested in being compensated for going that extra mile."

"They really don't want to attract people to come just for the money."

■ "I understand that, and I am sure they have some experiences with people who did just that. Let me demonstrate two details that make my situation different. First, I am not interested in moving because of the money.

The opportunity has to really grab me. Second, from day one they will see that I am adding value and any money they pay me will see dividends right from the start."

- "If that is their concern, we are on the same page. I am not interested in taking a new job just for the money. I really am looking for an opportunity where I can quickly demonstrate my value by obtaining measurable results. In that environment I am confident that the management would see my contributions and reward me accordingly."
- "For me, if the opportunity is a good one, the money will follow. That said, though, to me the pay level for the job is an indication of what value the organization gives it. I am hopeful that they will see fit to pay what the marketplace is currently paying for that exact position."

"At that compensation level, why do you want to leave your current employer?"

- "I am not sure I want to leave. When your firm called, your recruiter presented a very interesting scenario that described an organization in a growth mode that is trying to put together a team of superstars to take the company to the next level and they are committed to do what it takes to get there. That's what made me want to hear more, but don't get me wrong: I like my job a lot and it will take a lot to consider leaving."
- "I have learned the hard way that there are more important things than money. There are issues at the organization now that I was unaware of when I joined. Had I known then what I know now I probably would not have accepted the position. The situation has become so

personally unbearable that I am being very flexible about my next job, so needless to say the opportunity, and not the money, is my primary concern."

■ "The organization has gone into a strategically different direction, and the unit I am a part of is no longer an organizational priority. So, to stay longer will only be damaging to my professional career."

■ "The week after I arrived, my boss left. Since then, there have been many departures in many different areas. I think the reason they paid me so much is that they are having problems attracting people at my level and then getting them to stay. I realize that jumping for the money was a mistake I will not make again."

"Wow, this is quite a résumé! You have some really terrific experience. I am concerned that you are overqualified for the position we have available."

■ "Quite frankly, I knew that coming here. You are recruiters with a great reputation, so I was thinking and hoping that in addition to the position you described, you would have other assignments more suited to what my experiences have prepared me for."

■ "Since we are meeting, let me ask you what is it about what you see on my résumé that makes you feel I am overqualified? One reason I wanted to meet with you— and so I was delighted when you invited me in—was to work with you to see what my value is in the marketplace from your perspective, keeping in mind the specific positions that I have recently held and the organizations where I have been employed."

- "I know that, but I also know this is a tough job market. I have been fortunate throughout my career and have had a steady progression of increasingly challenging jobs and have been paid based on what I have been required to perform in each of them."

- "I am well past the concern for bigger and more challenging. The opportunity that I see here is one that will be at a salary level that is fair for what is required and needed. The result will be a win-win for us both."

- "First, due to my added depth of experience I will provide more insight into the position so that solutions with more impact will frequently result. At the same time, you will take me away from the added demands that each of my most recent experiences required."

- "You are right, and I am overqualified. I knew that when I responded to the ad, but I have been with some organizations of late that paid well in exchange for a lack of job security. At this point, I prefer what your organization represents and the potential it provides. If that means I need to prove myself once again before picking up where my current job has been, I am willing to first demonstrate what I can do for you."

Responding to Objections If You Are a Job Seeker Fifty Years Old or Older

"We are not in quite the same position as your last employer, so we are reluctant to consider paying the same rate for this job. Am I correct in assuming that you are also receiving a pension? Would you be willing to accept a pay level that takes your current pension into consideration?

- "Let me be sure I understand what you just said. You are suggesting that I add the amount of the pension I am being paid to the total you are willing to pay me so that the combined amount would total what I think I should be paid to perform the job we are discussing. Is that correct?" [He or she agrees.] "I don't think that's something I could agree to."

- "My employer [or union] has been very good to me. With the pension I currently receive, I am willing to be quite flexible and even accept less than my last pay level to work here."

- "My current employer does have a reputation for being generous in both pay and benefits to her long-standing employees; that reputation is accurate. I also know that this is a highly competitive marketplace, so I do not expect the same level of pay if you bring me on board here."

- "Before we discuss salary, let me mention that with my kids already grown and the house paid for, I feel I can be flexible with salary. If and when the time comes, I am sure we can arrive at a mutually acceptable number."

- "If you agree to offer me the job, I am sure that the money will follow. I have been through a lot of different jobs and have a lot of meaningful experience that makes me confident that I will be a key player for you. To me, the job is the most important consideration. As long as the pay level is fair, I assure you that I will take into consideration the total offer, and that means a big emphasis on the job itself."

Part Three

How to Negotiate the Total Compensation Offer: Salary, Benefits, and Perquisites

You will encounter many of the following comments from interviewers when you are negotiating the total compensation package. Use some of the suggestions as responses to these comments.

Responding to an Initial Offer

"We are pleased to offer you the position, and we are prepared to pay you a salary of $60,000."

- "Thanks so much for your offer. Based on what I have learned so far, I am confident I will quickly deliver real value and savings or revenue. From my understanding of the market, what you are expecting from this job, and the total compensation package that you offer for this position, I feel a base of $60,000, with a six-month review, is fair."
- "Thanks so much for your offer. Can you tell me more about the total compensation package, including not only base pay but incentives of a year or less, incentives of more than one year, benefits, and perquisites?"
- "I had been hoping to meet with someone from Human Resources to discuss each of the elements of the pay and benefits package that your firm offers before arriving at this point. May I ask that you either have a meeting scheduled for me or let me know whom I should contact to set up a meeting?"

- "I very much appreciate your offer. That said, let me give you my preliminary response. From what I understand of the position, I feel an offer of $60,000 is fair. At this point, I still know very little about what comprises the total compensation and benefits package, so I might want to adjust that amount after I have obtained the additional information."
- "Thank you for the offer. Are there opportunities for bonuses or any other forms of incentives?"
- "Thanks so much for your fair offer. This to me is a terrific opportunity, and I appreciate your selection. As sure as I am that I plan to accept the offer, I ask that you allow me to sleep on it."

"How quickly can we look forward to hearing from you and getting this resolved?"

- "Today is Thursday [or Friday]. I would appreciate it if you would let me have the weekend to consider what we have discussed and allow me until Monday to get back to you."
- "Today is Monday. Let me think about this attractive offer and if it is acceptable to me, and I will make a decision by Wednesday."
- "Today is Tuesday [or Wednesday]. Could I get back to you Thursday [or Friday]?"

"What is there to think about? We have been meeting with you for quite a while. Is there any surprise in our offer?"

- "There are no surprises here, and I really appreciate the package you have offered. I just feel that for all important decisions, they are best made when one has the opportunity to sleep on them."

- "I feel it is a professional response to not make such an important decision immediately but to ask for a brief amount of time to consider the situation once more and then make a final decision. I assure you that once I give you my word, I will not take it back."

- (Weaker option) "For all important decisions I always like to go to my wife [spouse/significant other/trusted adviser, whomever] before coming to a decision. I value her [his/their] opinions, and I will feel better with the decision I come to if given the opportunity to discuss it with her [him/them] first."

"If you don't accept now, we will withdraw our offer. Take it or leave it."

- "I am sorry that you feel that way. Since I had planned to accept and your offer is a fair one, it is not difficult for me to accept your offer now. Thank you very much. I accept."

- "Am I correct in what I just heard? Did you say that if I don't take your offer immediately, you will rescind it?" [Response: "Yes."] "What would you do if our roles were reversed?" [Response: "I would accept without hesitation."] "That is what I will do as well."

- "Thanks for your offer but if you insist that I accept right now without time to consider the total offer, I feel it would be wiser for me to decline."

Be sure to ask the following questions whether or not you are prompted by a question or comment from the person conducting the interview. These are important points to cover in the effort to get you the optimum total compensation package.

Asking for a Job Offer in Writing

- "Thanks for the offer. It is certainly fair, and I appreciate the speed with which you came to your decision. We haven't spent any time discussing benefits. While I'm waiting for your offer to come to me in writing, may I have a copy of the brochures describing the benefits that are offered to employees at my level so that when the written offer arrives, I can swiftly come to a decision?"
- "When might I expect to receive this offer in writing?"
- "Would you please put the offer in writing? Your offer is fair and I plan to accept, but I will delay discussing this matter with my current employer until I receive your offer in writing."
- "This is a very important decision for me, and I would appreciate receiving the job offer in writing, delineating the terms of employment, the starting date, and benefit eligibility."

If Written Job Offers Are Not Provided

- "I understand that it is not your procedure to make written job offers. If I write the terms down as I understand them, will you confirm them?"
- "I am sorry that you feel a written offer is unnecessary. I would prefer something in writing. In fact, I agree with you that a person's word is so important, especially in the

business world. The situation becomes challenging when either you get hit by the proverbial truck or, for whatever reason, later on you and I have a different recollection of what arrangements and discussions we have come to. I perceive the letter as just being a summary of what has been discussed so that neither of us will have to rely on our memories to ensure that the terms to which we have agreed have been met." [Be sure to pause and keep silent until a response follows.]

- "Thank you very much. It is an attractive offer. I would prefer that you put it down on paper. When do you need an answer? Let me review it and consider it briefly. I will let you know my decision within the next two days, if that meets with your approval."

Negotiating a Higher Salary

- "Thank for the offer. Is the salary negotiable?"
- "Thanks for the offer. I was hoping for the base to be higher. Although $58,000 is fair, I have two concerns. First, it is at the low end of the range based on what other companies in this area are paying for this job. Second, from where I am coming from and the experience I bring with me, I am confident that I will quickly demonstrate bottom-line results. I feel my anticipated level of performance should warrant a higher starting salary. Is your offer negotiable?"
- "Thanks for the offer, and I appreciate your timely decision in my favor. At the same time, I must admit I am slightly disappointed. From what we discussed earlier and your

comments on the value that you and the organization place on this job internally, I was thinking that a higher offer would be coming, if and when you decided to hire me. Could something more be done?"

- "I understand that you must compare what you offer to me with what you are currently paying employees in similar positions. However, you seem to be agreeing with me when you state that my salary may be less than should be paid out of a desire to be fair to internal employees. It seems now may be the right time to do something for all your employees instead of enhancing a situation that sooner or later may have serious individual repercussions for the organization. Perhaps consider a modest increase to help achieve parity for your loyal and highly regarded employees to address this issue."

- "Are you willing to consider alternative, financial (but with less cost impact), as well as nonfinancial, opportunities that will help bridge the gap between the level of your offer and the marketplace?"

Negotiating a Sign-on Bonus

- "I know that you mentioned financial considerations are a challenge for your organization right now, so it will be difficult for you to raise the salaries of all who are in positions that are below the current market rate. Let me ask you to help me get to a pay level that is more consistent with the current marketplace. My suggestion is simple: consider me for a sign-on bonus. That one-time payment will not incur future costs, since it will not become part of my base salary. Additionally it will not create an imbalance for those in similar jobs, and at the same time that bonus will offset the lower salary. I estimate that the gap between your offer and the market is $5,000 so that is my number."

- "Since our agreement about the sign-on bonus will be in writing, let me suggest that you make it an offer letter, even though you had said earlier that is not your practice."

- "Could this item be included in an offer letter, since you want to have a record of this portion of our hire agreement? Why not incorporate all the details, so that everything that we discussed could be kept together in one document that I would even sign and return, if you so wished?"

Negotiating a Bonus

- "Thanks for the fair offer. With all due respect, I feel that the pay rate you have included is really not at the level I was hoping for, based on the research I had done regarding both this position and similar jobs in this local area as well as by comparable information for the pay rates of your competitors. Will there be an opportunity for me in this position to receive any bonuses?"

- "Would you consider doing something with a one-time bonus this year—if, of course, I meet objectives we agree to? It would certainly be helpful to offset the lower base that you have offered, and I am confident that I will quickly add value so that you will see that I warrant the payment."

- "I understand that other new employees (at my level, if so) have also been given a bonus arrangement. May I request the same consideration be given to me?"
- "The bonus you have offered is appreciated but, in considering the entire compensation package, still seems a bit low given market conditions and the experience I bring. Can we consider a performance review in X-months to boost the overall package? "

Negotiating Options[1]

- "Thanks for the fair offer. Based on our earlier discussions, I realize that your organization is really not financially able to pay a higher base at this time. With a deeper understanding of the organization and the demands placed on the position I would occupy, I agree the base pay you mentioned to me is the right number at this time."

---

[1] An option in this context is the right to purchase one share of stock for a set price at some point in the future. The days available to purchase the shares are known as a "window." The metaphor of the window is used to illustrate the fact that the period when the window is open, is the time available to purchase the shares. There is usually a starting date and an ending date for the opportunity. When the last day passes, the window is shut and the options expire.

An example of a window is: "You may exercise your option to purchase shares after six months has passed from the distribution date but no later than one year after the distribution has occurred."

Options are a great vehicle for organizations that have stock and are publicly traded to offer incentives to employees who demonstrate that their individual performance is tied directly to the success of the organization. Individuals profit from options when they exercise their right at a time when the price of the stock exceeds the "strike" price of the option if they also complete the other side of the transaction and immediately sell the stock.

How to Negotiate the Total Compensation Offer

- "You also see, I am sure, that I am not a job changer and I consider any move 'for the long term.' I see enormous growth prospects for the organization at this time, and for those who are a part of it."

- "Since you need to be frugal with the base, may I suggest a boost in such a way that will not cost the organization any money and at the same time provide me with a clear line of sight between my efforts and individual performance and the performance of the organization as a whole? My suggestion is that you offer me options."

- "Thanks for your fair offer. I notice no mention was made of options. Are they offered as part of the package?"

- "Are options something you would consider, especially since we are a bit apart on the base?"

- "Let me just make the point that options would go a long way toward reducing the difference between what I think the position should be paid and what you have offered. Additionally, they represent a real opportunity to link my performance to that of the organization."

- "Thanks for your offer. Will options be included?"

- "I was hoping that options would be a possibility. I have to share with you that I feel your offer is not as good as what I feel the position should pay and what I anticipate will be the value of the contributions I make to the organization's bottom line. If you were to offer options, then I would feel that, even though the base would be below market, the offer would be acceptable."

- "If you are not including options and there is no other compensation element to consider, then I ask you with all due respect to review the base pay level to see if you could somehow agree to a higher amount, more in keeping with what the marketplace is offering at this time."

Negotiating a Shorter Review Period

- "Thank you. Can you tell me when will I be reviewed? Will I be given consideration for a pay increase at that time, assuming that my performance warrants it?"
- "Thanks for the fair offer. I had been hoping for a higher pay level based on what I bring to the job. What is your policy for salary reviews? Is there any opportunity to get an accelerated review if my performance warrants—and I am confident you will quickly see results—since I am being paid at a pay level below what I had anticipated and what the market is currently paying?"
- "If I deliver what I promise in the first six months, would you consider giving me a bonus as a one-time payment to make me whole, since my starting pay is below what I feel the position should pay?"
- "Thanks for your offer. As you are aware, I was hoping the starting pay amount would be higher. Since you are unwilling to compromise on the base amount, would you consider accelerating my review date and consider me for an increase, if warranted, at the end of my introductory [or probationary] period?"
- "Thanks for your fair offer. I still feel that I will perform at a level higher than reflected in the starting pay that you are

giving me. I have no problem with that. I do ask though that you review my performance after 90 days and, if you feel my opinion is correct, you make a pay adjustment at that time."

- "Comparing apples to apples, the base is definitely fair. If the guideline for six-month reviews were still operational, then this would certainly work. I am confident that in six months I will have quickly proven to be a valuable asset to the team. Would you be willing to include a six-month review as part of the offer?"

- "I appreciate the timely decision you have made. However, I have just learned in reviewing your merit pay program that I will be unable to be given consideration for a pay increase for 21 months. I am starting at a time of year when everyone is just about to get reviewed, and I will not yet be here a year when annual reviews are done the next time around, nine months from now. Therefore it will be nine plus twelve months before I have my first review. I have three suggestions to offset this disadvantage. First, increase the base by the amount I would have received, had I been eligible for review now—to keep me whole. Second, review me at the end of my probationary [or introductory period] and grant me the increase I merit, in line with those levels already used. Then consider me for an increase in line with your policy in nine months, when all employees are considered for their yearly annual reviews, on a pro-rata basis, again to allow me to not fall behind. Third, give me an adjusted base now with merit increase consideration, if performance warrants, when everyone else is reviewed in nine months.

Negotiating a Different Starting Date

■ "Thanks for the fair offer. If I understand you correctly, the reason that you are not able to pay more is due to your current employees in the same job, who have a lot of seniority, and are at the same level."

■ "You know I am disappointed with your offer, but I may have a way to be more satisfied. Let me explain. I am ready to come tomorrow if my employer allows me to, because I am really excited about the opportunity. I am not sure, though, that you are aware that if I were to come tomorrow, I would be leaving a lot of money on the table, because I am anticipating a bonus to be awarded next month, and the person still has to be an employee to receive it. If you allow me to delay my start date until the bonus is paid, then we both win. What do you think of my proposal?"

■ "I am pleased with your offer and look forward to joining the organization. We discussed start dates before we had discussed compensation and before I realized that I would not be earning at the level I had anticipated. I am currently taking job-related courses. If I leave now, during the middle of the semester, I will have to pay my own tuition, because my current employer has a policy that states you must be employed at the end of the semester to receive any tuition refund reimbursements. I would like to ask you to allow me to delay my start date to the end of the semester so that school will not be a distraction. (I know I really want to give myself 100 percent to this job.) By doing so, I will not be expected to pay the additional out-of-pocket expense that would be my responsibility if I were to leave before the end of the semester."

- "Thanks for your fair offer. As we have discussed earlier, I wish the base were higher. If you allow me to delay my start for seven weeks, that will allow me to be eligible for this year's profit-sharing payout with my current employer and that will help to offset the difference in salaries."

Negotiating Pay for COBRA[2] Coverage

- "Thanks so much for the fair offer. I need to mention something that I was not aware of when we were discussing pay and benefits. Here you require new employees to wait six months before they are allowed to enroll in the company's health benefits program. I was not anticipating this expense."
- "With the family coverage I currently have, with my current employer, I will have the opportunity to obtain continuing coverage for my family and myself, through COBRA, if I pay for it. For family coverage, my monthly premium will be $992.50. Would you be willing to reimburse me for coverage on the same basis you contribute to the premiums for your employees now?"
- "If you are unable to raise the offer on the base portion of my compensation package, would you be willing to pay my COBRA premiums until I am eligible for health benefits with your organization?"

---

[2] COBRA stands for the Comprehensive Omnibus Budget Reconciliation Act, a federal law that requires employers to allow departing employees to continue obtaining health insurance coverage, for 18 months after termination of employment, if the former employee is willing to pay up to 102 percent of the monthly premium.

Negotiating the Ability to Work from Home

- "May I suggest that you consider allowing me to work from home so that I may save some of the expense of commuting to work? With the salary you offered at a lower level than I had anticipated, that will help me to make ends meet."

- "To allow me to work from home what assistance will you provide? Will you reimburse me for things like a phone hookup, fax, and printer? What are your policies on reimbursement for phone and electricity charges?"

- "May I ask you to consider a proposal that will help to eliminate the difference in what you want to pay me and what I think I should be paid? My proposal is simple. Just allow me to work from home. If you would provide me with whatever I need to be able to do my job, that would go a long way toward meeting the goal of making me whole."

Negotiating Flexible Hours

- "Money does not mean everything to me. Also, let me say I really appreciate your offer. In an effort to show my interest in agreeing to a win-win situation, let me suggest that you allow me to work flexible hours."[3]

---

[3] If a job allows for flexible hours and the organization has a flexible hours policy, the organization has "core hours" where all are required to be present. For a day shift, these hours would usually be around midday (from 11:30 a.m. to 2:00 p.m., employees are allowed to come late and leave late (or come early and leave early), as long as their total workday totals eight hours.

How to Negotiate the Total Compensation Offer

- "Thanks for your fair offer. As you know, I was hoping for a higher base salary, and I know I will perform at a level that will prove it. That said, I am willing to quickly accept your offer if, as part of the deal, you permit me to work on a flexible hours basis. Since I am a single parent with primary care responsibility for my kids, if you allow me some flexibility in my workday schedule, I will prove to be more productive."

- "Thanks for your offer. I appreciate it and am glad to accept, even though, as I mentioned earlier, I was hoping for and felt that this position really deserves a higher starting salary. Let me suggest something that will both go a long way to helping me feel that the lower offer is given additional value and not cost you any additional money. I am an only child with very old parents, and the responsibility for their care falls on me. My request is that you allow me to be flexible with my work schedule so that I may deliver the results you expect from me in this job while at the same time having some latitude in working from nine to five each workday. As part of this request I would also hope that you would allow me to run out during the day to bring my parents to their scheduled medical and dental appointments, if I am unable to obtain appointments outside of my working hours."

- "Thanks for your fair offer. Before I accept, which I plan to do, I have one small request. I, like you, am a big believer in balance between work and family life. With that in mind, I want to share with you something on the personal side. Along with a great wife, I have three terrific kids who are very active in school and sports. My wife also works full time. She too has a very successful career and a demanding job. We try to respect each other's time and commitments, and we share our responsibility for being available for our kids. There are going to be times when I will be expected to attend a daytime parent–teacher meeting or school event in which my child is participating. In those circumstances, I would like, with your prior approval, to be able to attend. As part of that arrangement I would of course make sure that my work is not affected. In fact, on those days I would come early or stay late to ensure that I worked the same hours as my regularly scheduled workday."

Negotiating a Four-Day Week

- "I know you mean well. I also know that you would really like me to join your organization. I too would like to close this deal and come on board. There is, however, a concern on my part for making ends meet. I have a suggestion. If you allow me to work as a consultant and generate my own business one day a week, then we will both win. First, you will have a person who works four days but will get 100 percent results, since I am very results-driven and will do what I have to do in terms of nights and weekends to get the job done. You also benefit by allowing me to obtain additional income one day a week, since then you will not have to pay me additional sums that will create financial challenges for you."
- "Let me make a proposal. If I accept the offer you just made at the pay level you mentioned, let me ask you to

allow me to work a four-day workweek. That way, the difference between the pay I will be receiving and what I think I need to live will be made up when I supplement my pay from you with additional business I obtain from consulting assignments."

- "Looking at your current staff and production needs, it seems that everyone leaves early on Fridays and most vendors are not available either. I would prefer a four-day workweek, with Fridays off to meet my teaching schedule. Would you consider this arrangement to meet both our needs?"

- You know that I really want this job and am not concerned about the 78-mile commute each way. Let me ask though if there is an opportunity to consider a four-day workweek since Fridays appear to be especially challenging for the round trip.

Negotiating for a Laptop Computer, Cell Phone, and/or Blackberry

- "Thanks for your fair offer. I am going to accept. Before I do, however, please share with me the organization's policies regarding high-tech work tools. For persons in positions comparable to mine, does the organization provide a laptop, a cell phone, or a PDA such as a Blackberry?"[4]

---

[4] PDA is the acronym for personal data assistant, the term for a variety of handheld devices that provide a one-stop resource for all contact needs (names and phone numbers) and in more sophisticated versions such as the Blackberry, opportunities to send and retrieve e-mail messages from remote locations.

- "In my current job, my employer sees the value of high-tech handheld devices for enhanced individual productivity. They have provided me with a laptop, pager, and cell phone. I do not see that I will really need a pager in my capacity with your organization, but will I be provided with a laptop and cell phone?"
- "Before we close the deal, let me ask what is your policy regarding laptops and Blackberrys? Do you provide them for persons at my level?"

Negotiating Authorization to Attend Professional Gatherings Such as Conferences, Seminars, and Workshops

- "Before we conclude, let me ask what the company's policy is regarding attendance at professional gatherings. As part of my continuing effort to stay current and up to date with all that is going on in my field, I see that periodically I need to attend various conferences and workshops on an occasional basis. Will I be given the time off, and will I be reimbursed for all my expenses including for the cost of the program itself?"
- "Before we close the deal, let me mention that in the past I have been accustomed to receiving reimbursement for attending professional conferences and workshops. Will I be allowed to do so here?"
- "What is the organization's policy toward persons at my level attending various conferences and workshops? Will I be reimbursed for all reasonable expenses and program costs?"

- "I appreciate your offer. I also know that traditionally you all have not encouraged employees to attend professional conferences, seminars, and workshops. Before we conclude, will you consider reimbursing me for my occasional participation in a professional seminar or workshop?"

Negotiating Reimbursement for Professional Association Memberships, Certifications, or Journals

- "Does the company reimburse employees at my level for subscriptions and memberships to professional associations? In addition to my membership in the Society for Human Resource Management, as a member with current certification at the SPHR level, I need to retain my active membership status, which includes an annual subscription to *HR* magazine, and taking the recertification test every three years. Will the organization support that effort by paying for those expenses? At current rates, it amounts to approximately $325 per year, with the cost of recertification annualized and included in that figure."
- "I find that one journal, even though costly, is a must read and is very helpful to me in identifying trends and competitive threats. What is the procedure for getting approval for such an expense here?"
- "Throughout my career I have always found certain professional associations always to be a big source of ideas and leading-edge challenges. Annual membership is $2,000 per year, and there is also an annual conference

that pays for itself in referrals and network building. Will you agree as part of our deal to allow me to attend the conference on company time and reimburse me for all expenses? I would have waited to raise this issue and would have assumed responsibility for its expense, if necessary, but since we agreed to a low starting base I am hoping that you will agree to pay for these expenses, in part to offset my agreeing to accept a lower offer than I had anticipated."

Asking for a Contract

- "I appreciate your offer, and it addresses many details. With that in mind, since this is the entertainment industry, may I have a contract?"
- "I am sure you understand that I am taking great risk by leaving my current employer, where I could be financially secure for the rest of my career. I love the situation you describe, and I am looking forward to being a part of your team. I am confident that I will quickly be one of your key contributors. However, with the risk involved I am wondering if you would consider giving me a contract so that we both agree to share in the risk of this new arrangement."
- "You have been very generous with your offer and have included details that seem unique; I appreciate all that you have done. Since this, however, appears to me to be a unique arrangement, may I ask that it be documented in the form of a contract that could also include the noncompete, nondisclosure, and no-solicitation clauses that you were going to give to me separately?"

- "Thanks again for your offer. I am delighted to be your first chief learning officer. Since this is a newly created position I know that there are unique risks involved, as this is unchartered territory for both you and me. I also know that you are the organization's biggest advocate for what we both perceive to be an important position. At the same time, should the situation change—for instance, should you depart, the organization be sold, or the board decide on a different strategy—my situation might become precarious. I know that it is not your customary policy to do so, but, since this is really a special situation, may I have a contract?"

- "I appreciate your offer, which includes a generous relocation package. I am really looking forward to getting here so that I can start what appears to be the best opportunity for me and, from my perspective, for the organization as well. May I ask, since this offer requires me to make some major changes personally and professionally, that you give me a contract to identify in one document all that we have discussed? That way, there will be a complete understanding on both our parts of what is and isn't included in this arrangement?"

Securing the Promise of Severance

- "Before we conclude our discussion, there is one more matter I would like to discuss. At this time do you anticipate the possibility of a sale, merger, or any other change in ownership?" [Response: "No."] Thanks, your response is reassuring. At the same time, you will agree this is a very complicated marketplace, and unanticipated mergers and acquisitions are taking place at very fast speeds in an ever-changing environment. I will be a key performer, and if any of these unanticipated changes in ownership occur, my position could be eliminated through no fault of my own. Let me suggest that you agree to something that is not going to cost the company any additional compensation. Would you agree to provide six months' severance, with continuation of medical benefits on the same terms as I had been receiving as an active employee (not on a COBRA basis) in the unlikely situation that my job is eliminated due to any unforeseen circumstance such as the one I just described? If the basis for termination is for cause, of course, I would not expect any severance to be paid."

■ "There is just one more item. With severance, in the unlikely circumstance that our arrangement does not work out—for example, if you leave and your successor prefers to eliminate this position and save the salary expense, so that my position is eliminated due to no fault of my own—I would have a small financial cushion to help me through my transition to another job. They say now that people at my level in my profession take on average 10 months to find a job, so what I am asking for is 12 months' severance, including medical benefits, pre-COBRA."

■ "As we are about to conclude, there is one last item I would like to raise. Does your organization provide severance for employees at my level? (No.) Let me ask that you consider extending a promise of severance for this position. I don't anticipate having this happen, but you are asking me to leave a very secure situation with people who really appreciate the work that I am doing. I am very pleased with what I see here but I do know that switching jobs can be a major decision. You would help my comfort level with an agreement with which, if for whatever reason this does not work out, I would have something of a financial security net. That way, I would not be caught in a real cash-flow bind. I want you to also know that if the decision is based on just cause, I would not expect the severance agreement to be executed. I am more looking for this severance detail just to reassure myself that we are both committed to making this work and we are both sharing in the risk."

Negotiating Tuition Refund

■ "Thanks for your fair offer. Although I do really want to accept your offer, you also know that I wish that the position were paying more. I understand that you have your reasons for not raising the pay level, and I know too that you are unwilling to consider a faster review schedule and an up-front bonus. I am going to try one last avenue to see if there may be some movement in the total compensation package that will bring me closer to the level I was hoping for. I appreciate your willingness to listen to these requests, and I feel that you, just like I do, really want this deal to close. That said, I wonder if you would consider tuition reimbursement as a way to provide me with additional compensation at a reasonable cost to you."

■ "You may have no tuition refund policy at this time, but I would not be surprised if even without one, from time to time, you have supported your employees' education pursuits with reimbursements for tuition, books, and fees. Might you consider a more formal tuition reimbursement agreement as a part of your offer to me?"

■ "My current employer has a very good tuition refund policy, but as a result of my accepting your offer and the starting date you prefer, I will not be able to complete this semester's courses nor receive my tuition refund for this semester. What I am asking you to do is give me the tuition refund payment that I will lose by coming here."

■ "I know you have a tuition refund policy here, but there is also a one-year waiting period. As you know, I am currently attending school and receive tuition refunds from my employer. Would you be willing to allow me to receive tuition refund as soon as I start so there is no interruption in my school program?"

■ "You know I am currently attending school. Well, if I leave my current employer before the end of the semester, I will not be reimbursed for the tuition for this semester. Would you consider allowing me to change my start date? We are so close to the end of the semester that I would get here just three weeks later. Alternatively, would you consider reimbursing me—on a dollar-for-dollar basis— for my tuition expense for this semester?"

■ "I know that you are eager for me to start regardless of the tuition refund that I will lose at my current employer. I also know that you have a policy that tuition refund is only considered for employees who have been with the organization for a year or more. To get me here as quickly as you want and to keep your tuition refund policy intact, perhaps consider raising my base by just the amount of the tuition refund. It would go a long way toward making me feel that the offer is really fair, even though the actual dollars will not be as big."

Negotiating Child Care

- "You and I did not really agree on what this job is worth, and I accept your rationale. I do have out-of-pocket expenses that I need to consider, particularly since I am a single parent and am also my children's primary provider. I have learned that you offer Flexible Spending Account (FSA) arrangements, so I am pleased that if we come to terms, and I am really confident that we will, I will be able to pay my child-care arrangements on a pretax basis. On the other hand I still will have to come up with the money. Would you consider paying my actual child-care expenses? It would be a cost-effective way to meet halfway on our difference in base-pay level and come closer together on the total pay issue."

- "Thanks for the fair offer. I did not share this until now, but I feel this is the appropriate time. I have three kids and I am my children's primary care provider. To return to work and join you, I will have to make arrangements for my kids to be in child care. I need to be careful about where I put them, and I have found a facility that is ready to accept them, but as you may suspect, the cost is not insignificant. Would you consider an adjustment in my base pay to meet this expense? It would do two things. First, it would help me a lot and, second, it would not be as costly as the difference in base that I was hoping for."

■ "I appreciate your offer to have me join your organization. It is an exciting opportunity, and I am confident I can do a lot for you. As you also know, I was hopeful that the pay would be higher. May I ask you to consider something that would go a long way for me, psychologically as well as financially, in terms of bridging the gap? Here is my suggestion. For me to return to work, I need to be sure that my children are taken care of. Now, I have already arranged for them to go to an after-school program, so that I know they will be safe and engaged while waiting for me to pick them up. I was surprised to learn that the fees for the program represent a sizeable expense for me, and it is something I had not given enough serious attention to when I considered returning to work. You would really be helping me out by relieving some of this pressure by increasing my base slightly. That would offset this additional expense, and the amount would still be significantly below what I feel the job is worth, based on what I anticipate doing for you."

Negotiating Benefits

■ "I appreciate your fair offer. I was hoping for more, but the opportunity is an enticing one, and I look forward to working closely with you as part of your team. After reviewing your benefits program, I notice that what your organization offers is not at the same level as what I currently have. One big example is that I will have a $5,000 ceiling on annual out-of-pocket medical expenses whereas I now have a policy that caps out at $1,000. With three kids and a spouse, I could easily see hitting that level with just one emergency. Is there something that could be done with the base to offset this potential significant increase in expense?"

- "Thanks for your fair offer. We will get a lot done when we start working together. There is one more issue, though, that I wish to discuss before giving you what I anticipate is a favorable decision. Your health-benefits package is a little disappointing. In noticing the providers that are part of your HMO (health maintenance organization) network, there seem to be only a few from this area—and none that are known to me, my family, or my friends. So, it looks like I will need to take the more expensive "point-of-service" plan. The cost to me will be an additional $5,000 in annual premiums, according to your current schedule. Would you consider including that amount in my starting base, to make me whole?"

- "Before concluding and closing this deal, I need to raise an item that I discovered when meeting with your benefits manager. I just learned that my family and I will not be eligible for health insurance until I complete six months with the organization. When you and I discussed base pay, you will recall that I was hoping for a higher base pay amount. I was willing to take the lower amount, because I am excited by the prospect of working here. Now, however, I see that I will have to pay an additional $6,000 to continue my health benefits with my current employer through COBRA, until I am eligible for coverage here. Is there something you can do so that I do not have to pay $6,000 as part of my arrangement for coming here?"

■ "Your base pay offer is very generous. The one thing holding me back is the lack of health benefits for six months. It will cost me $6,000 for coverage until then. If I could have some support on that issue, I think we both would be satisfied."

Negotiating Additional Vacation Time / Time Off

Vacation

■ "Thank you. I also want to be sure you are aware before we proceed further, that I have been planning a trip to Spain that has been scheduled to take place from August 15 to August 30. I want to be sure it won't be a problem."

■ "Thanks for your fair offer. As you know, I am happy to join your organization, but I do wish the pay would be higher. Let me make a suggestion that will not cost you more money but that will be an effective way to eliminate the difference in what you will be paying me and what I feel the position should pay. My suggestion is a simple one. In addition to work, I also value my leisure time with my family. With that in mind, I propose that you allow me to take an additional week of paid vacation each year."

■ "I appreciate your offer, and am ready to accept. I need to bring to your attention a situation that I have committed to before we close this deal. Each year a group of my friends from the old neighborhood gather together with their spouses and families for a week at some remote location—the dates for which are booked far in advance. This year we had reserved the week of July 14 through the 21. I know those dates come up right after I begin working for you, so I do not expect to be paid, but I am hopeful that you will honor this request and allow me time off to attend this gathering. In future years it will not be a problem, because I will take the time as my regularly scheduled vacation."

- "Thanks for your fair offer. As we discussed earlier, I was hoping for a higher starting base, because of what I bring to this job and what will be expected of me. But I understand your reasons for paying at the level that you are. That said, I have a small request. My spouse and I had made plans to take a trip to Nantucket more than a year ago and if we are unable to go, we will lose our $2,000 down payment. The dates are August 12 through August 28. I know I have not yet accrued sufficient credits for time off, but I am hoping that you will agree to allow me to take the time off."

- "Thanks for your fair offer. I appreciate also your setting up the meeting with the benefits manager. One item that I had not given much attention to initially is vacation, but I am glad I did at the meeting. I need to share with you that for several years, and for more than one employer, I have become accustomed to annual four-week vacations. When I work, I really work, but then I need to recharge my batteries and spend some time with my family. Can anything be done to allow me to continue to have the same benefit here? I know that, having that time off, I will not perform less on the job but instead actually will perform much better as a result."

Sabbaticals

- "You know that the job I am accepting is a high-pressure one. I am confident that I will thrive in this environment. In the past I have been allowed to take time off as a sabbatical. Will I be offered the opportunity to do the same here?"

Time Off for Religious Activities

- "Thanks for your offer. There is one more matter I would like to bring up at this time. I am very active with my religious community. We all participate in a week-long retreat each year. With that in mind, may I ask you to consider my reasonable request for an additional week of annual vacation? This would certainly go a long way to resolving our differences on pay."

Counteroffers

Type A: A Second Level of Negotiation with Your Would-Be New Employer

- "I have to share with you an unexpected development. When I mentioned to my boss that I would be leaving, she disclosed that if I were to stay, there would be an additional $10,000 in my annual pay, three months from now. I am still certain that I am making a good move in joining your organization. I wonder, though, if, since you are aware I was hoping for a higher starting salary, you would consider doing something for me there. And if that is not doable, would you consider increasing my options grant?"

- "I have to share something that has come to me as a complete surprise. My current organization is really making it tough for me to leave. They have just asked me to stay four more weeks and will pay me a bonus at the end of it, if I agree to do it. Are you willing to allow me to delay my start?"
- "You know I am pleased with your offer. Now unexpectedly my current employer has upped the ante to match your offer. I do not want a bidding war to occur but felt I should share this latest development with you."

Type B: Negotiation with Your Current Employer

Consider the scenario where your current employer wants you to stay. The responses that follow are good ones you could use if you hear a comment like the one below.

"We don't want to lose you. We want to match or even would be willing to better the offer you just were given to induce you to stay. What will it take to get you to stay?"

- "I appreciate your interest, but while I have enjoyed working here, I cannot pass up the unique opportunity offered me by the other company."
- "I have decided to accept a position with the other company. You know that I like it here, but I received a phone call and, although I wasn't looking, I decided it would not hurt to hear what they had to say. Well, things really took off quickly from there, and before I knew it, they made me an offer too great to pass up, and here we are."

- "You know that I feel there are more important aspects than financial ones to consider when making a serious decision to change jobs. The financial elements, however, cannot be overlooked. The other company is offering 15 percent more than my current salary and a bonus potential of 20 percent. With my understanding of the budgeted merit pool here, it looks like my next merit increase in six months will more likely come in at 2 to 4 percent."

- "Even though you know pay is not my primary concern, the package of pay and benefits they put together is difficult for me to pass up, given my current situation [for example, a new baby, new house, new commute, or higher gas prices]."

- "I don't want to sound demanding, but you know I really do like it here. I owe it to you and me to consider anything you wish to offer me to reconsider. I need to ask you, though, if you could let me know when I may learn of your decision, since they are waiting for me to confirm a start date."

- "I am quite taken by your question. Thank you so much for demonstrating your interest in keeping me. You have really taken me by surprise. As attractive as the offer is that I have been given by the other company, I owe it to you and me to seriously address your question. Let me think about this overnight and get back to you in the morning."

- "You know that I am not basing this on going to the highest bidder. Although salary is something to keep in mind, I need to weigh the other factors that are really important to me, and at the top of that list are two. The first is the opportunity to continue to grow professionally, and secondly is the organization itself. Thanks again. Let's talk in the morning."

Dealing with Multiple Job Offers[5]

Suppose you have job offers from more than one company. What do you say to individual companies to help you make your decision? Below are some appropriate responses.

- "I am very excited about this opportunity. Your organization is one that I am really looking forward to joining. Is there anything that can be done to accelerate the process? Let me explain why. Out of nowhere, I received an enticing call from another recruiter. I was upfront with them and let them know that we were close to an offer, but I felt it would not hurt to see what they were interested in discussing. One thing led to another, and before I knew it they made me a written offer. You know that my strong preference is here with you, but at the same time I do not want to get my hopes up, since I am still waiting for a decision from you. Without sounding presumptuous, may I ask you if and when I may expect an offer from you?"

---

[5] Whether comparing your current job with one job offer or comparing multiple job offers, it is always important to look at all the factors, tangible and intangible. (See the worksheets that you filled out in Part One for your original list of Wants and Needs.)

- "I really am impressed with your organization. As you are aware, I have given my job search a lot of attention. As luck would have it, I am also close to an offer with another organization.[6] May I have until midmonth to make a decision?"

- "Although pay is not going to be the final determinant in my decision, another organization has offered me a base of $60,000, a sign-on bonus, stock options, a short-term incentive package, an accelerated review schedule, and immediate health-care coverage. I would prefer to work for your organization, but of course that other offer is quite attractive. Might you be willing to discuss similar terms?"

- "I do not want to be involved in a bidding war. The reason for my sharing information about other job offers with you is precisely because I take any job change very seriously. Let me remind you that the only reason we met is that your recruiter was so persuasive. I was quite happy with my job and organization. It was only when the name of your organization was disclosed and the job opportunity presented in detail did I feel that I owed it to myself and my family to pursue it at all.

Finalizing the Offer

The following are appropriate comments and responses for finalizing the offer, either accepting or declining.

---

[6] Do not reveal the other organization's name. Doing so would be too risky. In this very complicated marketplace, some employers just might rescind their offer to you if they knew you also applied to other companies for whom they do not have a high regard.

Accepting the Offer[7]

- "Thank you. I feel that we both have come out with a win-win situation. I appreciate your support and look forward to starting on October 15."

- "Let me be sure I understand the offer that you have so kindly just made. You have made me an offer to join you with the job title of Human Resources manager, reporting to the Human Resources director. Additionally, my starting pay will be $60,000 per year. The other terms include the following: I will be eligible to participate in your health-benefits program, starting on January 15. I will also be given a sign-on bonus of $10,000 that will be paid in two installments. The first will be processed my first day of work, and the second will be paid after I complete my first three months of employment, which also coincides with the end of my introductory/probation period. There will also be a three-month performance review that I will receive at the end of my introductory/probation period. This determination will include consideration for a merit increase. I understand that, based on current policy, going forward I will receive performance reviews and merit increase consideration on the anniversary date of each year of my employment. Based on the level of my position, I will also be given a vacation of three weeks annually, that will start to accrue from my first day of employment. So my first year's entitlement will be 15 days, to be taken after six months of service, with prior

---

[7] Always follow-up with a written acceptance and thank you. Sample letters are provided in Part Five.

approval from my supervisor. You also agreed to provide a laptop and Blackberry. Did I omit anything?"

■ "As we discussed, please do not contact any references with my current employer until after I give you my decision. I will inform you of my decision as soon as I receive the written offer. I will also submit my resignation at that time. When may I expect to receive this offer in writing?"

Declining the Offer

■ "I appreciate your good-faith efforts to resolve this situation, but as tempting as the offer is, I do not feel that this is the direction my career is heading at this time. If the situation changes, I hope we can speak again in the future."

■ "Thanks so much for your fair and timely offer. I really appreciate all the interest and attention you gave me during this exciting time. Due to circumstances that are difficult to describe in detail, I feel it best to decline your offer at this time."

■ "Please allow me to ask you to keep the door open and if and when my situation changes, I hope that you will reconsider my strengths and recall our discussions from this time to see if you would like to extend an offer to me at that time."

■ "To work with you as you go through this next challenging phase of the new-product rollout would be a unique and challenging opportunity. At the same time, however, I do not feel that I would be able, with my personal commitments, to give as much as it appears the position will demand of me."

- "While I must decline this offer now, let me ask you to allow me to apply again for a job at your organization at a future point in time. You already know that my feelings for the organization, the job, and the person to whom I would report are all so positive, yet to leave my current employer at this time would present challenges for an organization where I have already invested so much time and energy. So, I feel it is not appropriate for me to leave at this time. I hope you see in this action some indication of the person that you would be gaining if the timing were better."

If You Do Not Get a Job Offer

And if, even after all that effort, you don't get a job offer? The following are appropriate responses.

- "Even though I feel that my skills, experience, and enthusiasm are a great match for the position, I do recognize the competition to work here. I wish you and the chosen candidate much success, and if there is another position where you feel my résumé is a better match, I hope we can talk again."
- "I was sorry to learn that I will not be joining your organization at this time after all. I appreciate the opportunity to be considered, and the more I got to know your organization, the more I wanted to become a part of all that you are doing. Please extend my appreciation to all those who contributed to the professional time and courtesies given to me. The hospitality displayed by each and every member of your organization is something that I will remember for a long time to come."

- "Please know that if I you ever consider reopening our conversation, I welcome your doing so. It would be an honor to be considered once again."

- "Thank you for considering me, and let me also extend my personal wishes for continued success in all that you do professionally."

- "Thank you for conveying what to me was very disappointing news. It was quite an adventure to have the opportunity to know more about what you all are doing. The more I saw of your company, the more I realized that you all are a truly unique bunch, possessed with enormous talent, a purposeful resolve, and a sense of urgency, which I have rarely found elsewhere."

- "To see all that you wanted me to see and then to be let down with your decision to make the offer to another candidate was a setback for me, to be sure. Please be aware that, even though I have not been offered a job at this time, I would certainly be willing to go through the process again. The risk of another rejection at the final stages would be worth it, just to see if the next time I am more successful in landing a job in what appears to me a dream organization. All the best to you and your team. I hope we get the chance to work together soon."

Part Four

Negotiating at Your Current Job

Performance Reviews

Phrases for Discussing Performance

"How did you think you did this past year?"

Here, you need to name two or three of your best achievements and quantify them when possible with numbers (percentages and/or amounts). By doing this, you are framing the discussion by finding out up front if your supervisor is in agreement that you had a great year. If so, then you are planting the seeds for what should be a great increase. If your supervisor does not agree with you that you had a great year, then it's better to know this sooner rather than later, because it may be a predictor that your salary increase is not going to be so good, if you are getting one at all.

- "I had what I consider a terrific year. In addition to the project, I also am proud of my other accomplishments, namely . . ."
- "I had a great year. I completed the installation of the _____ software package on time and within budget. I trained Jon, Mary's replacement, so that we were able to save the difference in her salary and his— approximately $10,000 annualized—without missing a business beat and meeting production requirements as well."

■ "Even with challenging market conditions, I met sales targets the first and third quarters and exceeded those targets in both the second and fourth quarters—by 20 percent in one and 37 percent in the other, for total orders of $650,000 above target. Additionally, I found the time to participate in two national conferences that, even though they haven't yet led to increased sales, will do so next year. I am confident of that. In fact, as I shared with you earlier, I am in serious conversations with two prospects right now that should in the next 90 days lead to a contract."

■ "I thought we had a pretty good year. We hired 103 persons to fill both vacancies and new positions. Our cost-per-hire expense was 5 percent below last year. The time-to-fill number dropped by four days, from 32 to 28. Let me also mention we spent $180,000 less this year in recruiting fees than last year."

Ask Your Employer, "How Do You Feel I Did?" Then Listen Carefully to His or Her Response before Replying

■ "Thanks for your frank comments. I know you have a lot on your mind, and my goal of bringing only solutions to you sometimes may get lost in the fray. I really do appreciate these sessions as an opportunity to reflect on what has happened. I also like the opportunity to see if my efforts will be recognized with an annual increase, not to mention promotion."

■ "I appreciate the time you give me at these annual sessions, and I like to think about my accomplishments over the year. I feel I also need to put them in writing for you to review before we meet, just to confirm that what I thought was a pretty good year, you do as well."

- "I know with you stretched so thin we don't get to meet frequently to discuss my performance. Let me ask you now before we start, did I meet your expectations this past year?

Be Ready for Any Comments That Are Intended to Weaken Your Accomplishments

Your Accomplishment: "Even with light TV ratings, we were able to fill the Alamo Dome with 50,000 people."
Weakening Remark: "It seats 60,000, and you did have to give away a lot of $5 seats."
Affirm Your Accomplishment: "I did not want to book the Alamo Dome. You did. The total population of San Antonio is just 250,000. We attracted 25 percent of the entire population for this event. Are you saying that that was not such a great challenge?"

Phrases for Salary Review

After the discussion of performance passes, it is time to turn to the aspect of the meeting known as the "salary review" (frequently also referred to as "merit pay"). More astute organizations realize that to combine the topics of performance and increases is to risk forgetting the entire discussion of performance, as the employee just wants to find out what his or her increase will be. Most, however, still combine them.

If your organization combines them, be attentive to the first portion of your review, as discussed above, to look for clues for what you may expect during the pay portion. If your supervisor praises your performance, be gracious and then remember those comments to make an argument for a higher increase during the second portion. Be sure to refer to the section on "Understanding How Compensation Works" in Appendix A before you begin negotiating your compensation.

What follows are what might be comments you'll hear about salary increase—and appropriate responses to them.

"We are quite pleased with your work and will be giving you an increase of $3^1/_2$ percent this year."

- "Thanks for sharing my increase with me. I know you try to be fair, but I am concerned that with the budget you had to work with, I am really not keeping up with increases in the cost of living that affect me and my family personally. Additionally, I know that if I walk out the door, it is more likely that I would be paid more than I would for staying here. Now, I know no one is indispensable, but does it make sense to encourage me to leave and take all that I know about this place along with my proven skills? If that were to happen, you would have to pay more to obtain a person at a comparable experience level to get what you did when I was in the job. Why not make the whole solution much simpler and pay me what someone else would?"

- "Thanks for the fair increase. I am concerned, though, that, with the budget constraints and the decisions you are forced to make, those who are here longer and making bigger bucks get the bigger portion of what is a very limited salary budget. Now, according to you, I am one of your key players, and yet I have to live with this arrangement and it doesn't look like my predicament will change anytime soon if I stay with this organization."

■ "Thanks for the pay boost. An increase of 10 percent will take me near my maximum for this position. What do you suggest my next move should be?"

"This has been a tough year for us. Although you have done a terrific job, we will only be able to give you an increase of 3 percent."

■ "I understand, and I appreciate your comments, but perhaps there may be other ways that will make this situation acceptable . . ." [Offer some alternatives such as new computer, new office, tuition refund, telecommuting, a four-day workweek, an extra week of vacation, permission to attend a convention, start/continue a degree program that they will subsidize either in time off or by paying the school directly, a promotion.]

■ "I understand that not only were you limited by the small budgets you were given to work with this year, but I know you are also locked in because of where my pay level is in the grade that I am in. But I have to say, though, that in doing my research prior to today's meeting I find that in this area people who are doing the same job as me are averaging a pay level, even with my projected increase, at $10,000 more than I am. Could I suggest that the job be reevaluated?"

If the Increase Is Unacceptable to You

■ "This is not acceptable. Can anything be done to improve it?"
■ "My research indicates that my pay level is not keeping pace with the marketplace. With the increase you are offering me, I will fall farther behind. Is there something that you are not telling me?"

There is a risk that the conversation will turn more serious here, but you should want to know if something is going on of which you're not aware. If nothing is wrong, then you need to know the real reason why, if your work is considered valuable, you are not getting more of an increase.

- "I am aware that you and I have our differences, but I believe that you like my work and I know I like this organization. But please understand that while I would prefer to stay with the company, at the same time I know I could do better financially if I were to go outside. Please be open and share with me your opinion of what I should do."

- "I am hearing you say that you like my work, but at the same time you are agreeing that my performance is not rewarded with the pay increase you are offering. If you were in my shoes, what would you do?"

- "I understand the constraints you are under, as my manager. However, I know too that frequently current employees are taken for granted with small increases or none at all, especially since there is a perception that there are many more people out there looking for jobs than there are jobs. I also know that when the organization has the opportunity, they like to go after fresh talent in the marketplace. Now, in doing my research, the conclusion I draw is that I am already slightly underpaid, and with the small increase you mentioned, I will fall even farther behind. Let me also ask whether you are also stating that any new hires will be brought in at higher salaries. If so, then employees like me have two issues to address: first, current incumbents in the job are not being paid what the organization should pay them, and, second, the organization is willing to pay more for outside, untested talent than it is for the employees it already knows. Does that make sense? Is there anything you can do to change it?"

How to Ask for a Raise or Promotion

At the Completion of a Project

- "Hi, Jack. What do you think of this project that we have just completed?" [Let him speak, and listen carefully. If his response is negative, you need to determine the reason(s) for his opinion and whether he has any concerns about your performance. If so, those need to be addressed before you continue the conversation that follows. If his response is positive, continue.] "I too am impressed, not just with the fact that we have successfully completed this project but how we accomplished it. I feel so good about this important undertaking that I am hoping you will consider an increase for me at this time. The fact that I actively participated in every aspect of this project did not affect all the other responsibilities that were part of my everyday activities and had to be completed as well. Do you agree that I am deserving of a raise at this time?"

- "Hi, Louise. Thanks for agreeing to meet with me. I wanted to meet with you while this project's completion is fresh on everyone's minds. Please share your comments about this accomplishment." [Then after she does . . .] " Now, how do you feel about my contributions in the successful completion of this project? "[If the response is positive . . .]" "I have to share with you that I feel very good about what I have been able to do, and I will always be grateful to you and the organization for allowing me to be part of the great team we had. But I do feel that a reasonable form of recognition for all the effort I displayed on this assignment is a pay increase. How do you feel about my suggestion?"

■ "Hi, Alison. Thanks for meeting with me today. I can just imagine how far behind you must be with so many responsibilities that had to play second fiddle to the time you needed to spend on this project. I have the same challenge, although I am sure many fewer than you. By the way, I really appreciate the kind mention you gave me when identifying key players at our post-project completion celebration. It meant a lot to me. That comment, though, triggered a thought in my mind. If I have really demonstrated what I could do when called upon to do so, I hope you will give me the opportunity to contribute at that level again sometime soon. If I am so highly regarded in the organization, let me also ask that you give me a pay increase at this time, since I haven't had one since last August, and at that time budget constraints limited the increase to just 4 percent."

Because of Market Conditions

■ "Hello, Frieda. Thank you for agreeing to meet with me today. I know you squeezed me into your tight schedule, and I appreciate it. Let me get right to the point. It appears that our organization has not kept pace with the market when it addresses salary levels for positions in your department. Here is some information that I have obtained to demonstrate this point. "[Here, you provide copies of salary survey data that you obtained from the Internet, newspaper ads, and job postings]. "Further, I know that some of us are starting to get calls from recruiters, and their enticement is a much bigger financial opportunity—we are talking a pay difference of 25 percent in total compensation, including bonus incentives and option opportunities. I want to be sure you are aware of this before you start to lose your staff, one by one. We have been really lucky with our staff and have had hardly any turnover, but it also has been quite a while since our last pay increases, and, when we did get them, they were none too generous. I suggest you speak to the folks in Human Resources to alert them and see if they would consider a market adjustment at this time."

- "Thanks, Alex, for agreeing to meet with me. I will not take a lot of your time. I need to let you know that I have been approached by a recruiter who is trying to entice me to consider a job with a competitor with a package that amounts to the opportunity to earn 25 to 40 percent more in the next 12 months. Now, I was not at all tempted, but if what she indicated was an accurate pay level for a job that is similar to what I am doing here, then it seems that our pay levels—at least for this position—may no longer be market sensitive. Do you think something could be done to investigate more fully and, if my information is accurate, consider me for an increase, to bring me closer to the market at this time?"

- "Hi, Jose. Thanks for today's meeting. I have a moderate concern that I feel you should know about. One of my neighbors happens to be a recruiter in my profession. Last weekend when we ran into each other she asked me some direct questions about how I was doing professionally. In the course of the conversation, the topic of salary came up, and she was quite surprised that I was not making more in this position. She started me thinking about the last few increases that I have been given and the budget constraints that you have been working under. It seems like I am being penalized for being a devoted and loyal employee because I have stayed here for so long. She made it sound like if I had been more of a job hopper, I would now be at a much higher pay level. That just doesn't sound right. You and I have a great relationship. I am confident that you value my work performance and I trust you and enjoy being a member of your team. But let me ask you to see if there is any merit to her comments. I know that if you find she is correct, you will do what you can to reduce or even eliminate the difference. When shall I follow-up with you? "

Because of Personal Issues

■ "Hi, Lucille. Thanks for agreeing to meet with me on such short notice. You have always made me feel comfortable bringing up anything with you that I need to, whether it is work related or not. Today I need to bring something to your attention that is a bit of both. As you know, my eldest kid is turning 16 and we have had plans for ages to celebrate in first-class style, and it is costing us plenty. Well, while staying focused on that situation, we did not realize that her school would also be closing. Now, there is only one school that we can consider for her as an alternative and that is the Taft School in Watertown. What that means for us is that we will have to come up with tuition and transportation costs of approximately $10,000 for each of her remaining two years of high school. Is there something—anything—the organization can do by way of a pay increase to make the whole obligation more manageable?"

- "Hi Larry. Thanks for agreeing to meet with me today. I have a personal problem, and I wonder if you will be able to help me out. You know that I have been going through a difficult divorce. You know too that I sometimes wonder if my attorney is sometimes being paid by my ex-spouse, from the positions he takes that frequently do not seem to be in my best interest. This divorce is going to take every last asset I ever owned—whatever of value I used to possess, my spouse seems to claim as hers. Recently, I received a decision on monthly child-care allowance, and that was the last straw. In doing the math, a bare-essentials budget makes me short on a monthly basis by $542. Could the organization see fit to help me to meet some or all of this difference with an increase in pay at this time? I know I should not bring my personal problems to work with me, but I also know from our relationship that you always want to know about what is on my mind, even if personal, when I wish to share it. It is this confidence that brought me to see you today."

- "Hi, Jack. Thanks for this meeting on such short notice. I will get right to the point. My car has finally died. It lasted longer than both you and I thought it would, so I can't complain. Now, however, I need another car fast, so I can get to work when I am supposed to. As luck would have it, I have a neighbor with a terrific car who is interested in parting with it, and I know she also feels for me since she is giving me the car for below red book value. The only problem is that she needs cash for a down payment for her new car, so she is counting on me. I know this is a reach, but would you consider giving me a pay increase, since I am due for one shortly anyway? Alternatively, would you consider giving me a cash advance against the increase so that I would have enough to buy the car? You could deduct the difference in pay each pay day until I have paid back the entire cash advance."

Because of Internal Inequity

■ "Hi, Joan. I really need to speak to you, so I appreciate your willingness to meet with me on such short notice. My issue is simple. Today at the water cooler I inadvertently overheard my newly arrived colleague, Monique, talking about her pay rate and, if what she said is accurate, she is making $5,000 more than me, even though she has less experience than me and she just got here. I know that I have been here a while, and I know that frequently the market for talent keeps going up outside the organization and that it is driven by so much turnover in my profession. Why else do people agree to take another job if not for substantial increases in pay? I know you always like to be fair to us employees in your department. Can you do something to correct this pay inequity?"

Negotiating at Your Current Job

- "Hi, Oliver. Thank you for meeting with me today. I want to bring something to your attention that you may already know about and are already addressing. Even though we and the shipping department have identical jobs, it seems that something has occurred that has resulted in higher pay grades for them than us. As annoying as that is, it is even more so since I learned, while discussing another topic, that they are also being paid at a higher level (in some cases it sounds like 25 percent more). I felt you should know about this, in case you already didn't. Better to hear it from your staff firsthand. Knowing you, I am sure that, unless there are other factors we are not aware of, you will make a case for an increase for our group, if you determine that we are not being treated equally. This does not seem to be an intentional slight, though. You and I both know that they have had a lot of turnover. When you have to go outside to buy talent, you will always have to pay more. But that consequence is not one we should be penalized for, because we have been the ones to stay put and really put our best selves into the growth of this organization."

- "Hi, Louise. Thanks for today's meeting. You always tell me that if anything is bothering me, you want to know about it, so here I am. You know how much I enjoy being with this organization and how much I like working for you. You know too that whatever you give me to do, I gladly do it, since I want to be very much a team player. You know also that I am not the most aggressive employee when it comes time to tooting my own horn; in spite of that fact, I summoned up enough courage to meet with you today.

My request is a simple one. I am concerned that with all the responsibilities that have been added on to the full-time job I started with, my pay has not kept pace. I would like you to review what I am doing now and compare that level of responsibility with what you originally hired me to do. I am not complaining. I am only asking you to review the two different levels of my responsibility and see if the job with me in it is in fact a different job from what had originally been intended. If what I suspect is true, then I would ask that you consider me for a salary increase based on that higher level of responsibility."

If You Have Received Another Offer

■ "Thanks, Catherine, for agreeing to meet with me today. I hate bringing this up on the last day of work for you before your vacation starts, but I feel you would rather hear this from me directly. You know I really like working here and being part of your team. There is nothing I would not do for you. All you ever have to do is ask. Out of the blue, a recruiter called me, and I reluctantly agreed to meet with him. I really like being here, but he said it would not hurt just to listen. Well, the picture he portrayed was so compelling I felt I owed it to my family to learn more. One thing led to another and before I realized it I was given a firm written offer that includes a total pay package with an upside potential of 40 percent. Now, you know I have thought for quite a while that our pay levels here have not been keeping pace with the market for talent outside. I guess this experience proves the point. I really would prefer to stay and keep my job here, but I also need to meet my financial obligations. Is there anything that you would be willing to do to offset the wide disparity in what I am being paid here and what the other company is offering? I don't want to get into a bidding war and do not even expect you to match their offer. But at the same time I am hoping you make my decision an easier one. The fact that I just received an increase and will have to wait 18 months for the next one is certainly part of the impetus that made me request today's meeting. When may I expect to hear from you?"

- "Thanks for agreeing to meet with me today, Anthony. I am sorry to bring something of this nature to your attention, but I also feel you would rather hear it from me first. You are well aware that I have been thinking of going into business for myself for a long time but haven't had the capital or the willingness to take the risk that such a move requires. However, now my brother-in-law has come up with the cash and would like me to quit to devote myself full time to a new venture. As hesitant as I have been, I also know I am being hit with additional expenses now that the kids are growing up and my wife has lost her job. I figure it is now or never, since I am no longer able to live on the salary I am currently making. You know I love you and the company, but I need to go where I have the potential to earn as much as I can. I know there is a lot of risk even doing this, but I can no longer make ends meet with my current salary, even with the last increase, and I know full well there is the possibility that I will not have an opportunity to get another increase for at least 11 more months. You know that I would prefer being here for a variety of reasons, one being the job security. If only you could do something to get me to where I need to be with my take-home pay. The difference is not that much—approximately $750 per month—and it would make a big difference. My brother-in-law is pressing me for an answer. Would you be able to give me an answer, either way, by this Friday? Let me tell you, I really appreciate your concern and giving me the time to discuss this very important matter today."

- "Hi, Alice. Thanks for seeing me on such short notice. I have a dilemma that I wish to discuss with you. I value your opinion and I really need your advice. A good friend of mine has come up with a very unexpected and attractive offer. She wants me to join her at a mature organization that is trying to make bold initiatives to recapture market share and she wants to pay me $65,000 annually to take away any doubts I may have about leaving here, since she knows how much this organization and working for you both mean to me. What should I do? My instinct tells me to stay, but you know I also feel that my pay has not kept pace with the market of late. While I would have to wait probably until the end of my next review period here—nine more months—and it probably would mean that my increase would not exceed 3 percent, the same I was given at my last review, even though the CPI[1] has risen more than 3.5 percent, and that's not counting increases in gas prices. Could you do something for me by way of an increase now, to make my decision to stay here an easier one? How quickly could you let me know?"

---

[1] The Consumer Price Index (CPI) is the month-over-month comparison in changes of a basketfull of commonly purchased goods and services that serves to determine the rate of inflation or its alternatives (stagnation and deflation).

If You Suspect Another Person Has Been Hired to Replace You

- "Hi, Mona. Thanks a lot for agreeing to this meeting. There is a concern—I'm hoping this session will reveal whether it's well-founded or not—that Maria has been hired to replace me. I may be way off base: please let me know if I am. I know you made me acting manager when Joe left. You had said you were not sure that I had the depth to perform in that function but you wanted to give me the opportunity to find out. At the time you also mentioned that you needed to do "due diligence" and wanted to make sure that you looked at potential applicants from outside before coming to a decision. Not long after, Maria was hired to fill a new position as part of my team. Now I am hearing from the grapevine that she has been brought in specifically to fill the role of manager and the decision will be announced soon. If what I am hearing is true, I have no problem taking a subordinate role once again, but I would really hope that you all would recognize my willingness to be professional and act the "good soldier" by granting me an increase to help me see that you all recognize this is not the easiest thing for anyone in my shoes to accept."
- "Hi Harry. Thanks for agreeing to meet with me so quickly. I will get right to the point. I am hearing that it will be shortly announced that Louise will take over the role of manager for my department—the position that I have been filling in for these past eight months. I certainly am disappointed by your decision, but that is your call, and to discuss it from that perspective is not why I wanted to

meet with you. I am more interested in discussing with you the terms on which we agree to go forward. I am always a real professional and team player. I also feel this matter might have been better handled by bringing me into the process sooner. To hear about this from the grapevine is not really best for anyone involved nor for the organization. I am willing to stay for as long as you wish to ensure that Louise makes the transition in the most effective manner, but for doing so I would like to be compensated for performing above and beyond what is reasonable to expect. I see two elements in this compensation adjustment. First, an increase to my base at this time. Second, a bonus payment to be paid at the end of this assignment as a reward for staying up to the date that you feel my services will no longer be required."

■ "Thanks, Millie, for meeting with me today. You know that I always bring things to your attention whenever I feel you should be informed. You make me believe that that is the approach you prefer. Well, today I learned from my sources something that I would think you would have brought up with me first. I have been told that Javier has been hired as the assigned manager to replace me in my role as acting department head. It could have been better handled, but be that as it may, that is not my reason for raising the issue. I am bringing it up at this time to see what the best way to address this matter is, assuming that you want me to stick around to assure an orderly transition. What are your plans and intentions, and how do I fit into this picture or not—and, if not, how will you address my situation? You have to know that based on our relationship, this is really an unanticipated happening and

I have been blindsided by your course of action. If I am not to be included in your plan going forward, you need to know that it will take me quite a while to find another job. That said, I hope you will provide a severance package that will be fair, especially in light of my situation and willingness to be selfless in doing whatever the organization asks of me."

Asking for a Promotion

Following a Compliment for Good Work

- "Thanks so much for the compliment. I have to ask you while you are so positive with your feedback, is there any opportunity for promotional consideration at this time? This project shows what I can do if afforded the opportunity to deliver. I certainly want to do more, and I am hopeful that as your sign of good faith a promotion to regional manager will take place."
- "Thanks for your feedback. If you are so positive regarding my performance, is there any opportunity to be considered for a promotion to assistant director of marketing at this time?"
- "I know you appreciate my work. I have been in my current position for quite a while, so let me ask you, is there any hope for a promotion at this time?"

If The Person Leaves Who Was Occupying a Position That You Want

- "Thanks for agreeing to this meeting. The reason for it is to discuss the changes in responsibility in our department when Mary leaves. I want you to know that I am more than willing to take responsibility for those portions of her job that include trafficking, quality control, and cost estimating. In exchange for the increased responsibilities, I am hopeful that you will recommend me for a promotion to production manager."

- "Hi, Joe. I hear that Louise is leaving the organization. Have you given any thought to her replacement? I have. How about me?"

- "I know that Luke's leaving is putting you in a bind. I have a suggestion that will be a real solution to your replacement concerns: put me in his position. By doing so, you will have a proven quantity that will immediately be able to take responsibility for that position and allow you to consider and give attention to the variety of other matters that you are addressing right now."

If Your Supervisor Is Leaving

- "Helen, I just learned that you are leaving for a fantastic opportunity. I am amazed that they were unable to retain you with a counteroffer. We always worked so well together, and more than once you suggested that I be given a promotion before you leave. Is that something I will see before your departure?"

- "Henry, thanks for agreeing to this meeting. Louise knows that I asked to meet with you. In fact, she encouraged me to do so. With her imminent departure, you will, I assume, start a search for her replacement. Let me suggest a quick shortcut to a resolution: promote me to her position. I will be able to assume her responsibilities immediately, and you know what I am capable of doing. If you have any doubts, let me suggest you appoint me as the interim replacement while you search outside. I have no problem with that, and if you find someone you think will be stronger in the role, I will not take it personally."

- "Thanks, Larry, for meeting with me. I have just learned that Francine is leaving for a great opportunity. The grapevine is also saying that you have already decided to go with Sam. He is a fine employee in my opinion, but I am also of the opinion that before you make you final decision you consider at least one other internal candidate: me."

When a New Supervisor Arrives

- "Thanks for your time. I am delighted to be meeting with you one on one. With all that you have going on, I have to give you one more issue that you have inherited. It should have been resolved before Pauline left her office and the organization—the issue is me. For more than five years I have been in the same position. Before Pauline left the organization, she recommended that I be considered for a promotion. I don't know how far it got and that is why I am here today—to let you know what was left on the table before your arrival."

- "Thanks for agreeing to meet with me. I want to be sure that you know I am excited by your arrival. New blood is always good for an organization, and your background appears a terrific fit for what this organization is trying to accomplish. Let me know if I may be of assistance to you in any way. Let me also be sure that you are aware of my unique status. Although I am currently listed as an assistant editor, I had been assured before John left that once his replacement arrived I would get the promotion that had been promised a while ago. You will quickly see that I am performing all the duties of the function. I encourage you to talk to all the people with whom I interact on a daily basis. I am looking forward to your decision."

- "I know you met with Alice before she left to ensure a smooth transition. I don't know if she had the opportunity to discuss her recommendation for my promotion to you. Let me give you a brief summary of the background."

If You Just Think It's Time

- "Frank, thanks for agreeing to today's meeting. Let me get right to the point. As you know, I have been performing the same job for more than two years. You give me very good reviews, and I have other indications that you like my work. I am accurate, am I not, in how you feel about my work? I feel that with all the changes that have been taking place around here, it is time for me too to be considered for a promotion to marketing manager. Please share with me what you think of my proposal."

- "Thanks, Anne, for today's meeting. Lately, you have been more busy than usual, so I appreciate the time you give me today. With all that is occurring inside the organization, I was hoping you would share with me frank comments regarding my performance. I have taken on extra responsibility lately, and I love to do it: I feel it is just one more indication of how well we work together and what I am capable of doing when called upon. I am asking you to consider me for a promotion, since it seems that this new level of responsibility will be something that I should be expected to do as we move forward. All I am asking is that some recognition be given to me with the promotion since it seems the right time to do so."

- "Thanks, Frank, for this meeting. I will be brief. We get along and have for quite a while. I am always there when you need me. But you know me, and I am not one to toot my own horn. For the past several days I have been thinking about my future here. I really like this organization and working with you and the rest of the team. But I feel that sometimes I am taken for granted. Usually I don't mind, since I am a very low-maintenance employee, but I do think it is time for a promotion. It has been a while since the last one, and I do see others in other departments who started with me, passing me by as they move up the ladder. Would you consider a promotion for me at this time?"

If You're No Longer Feeling Challenged

- "Thanks for today's meeting, Jane. I have to tell you that recently I have not been challenged by my work and I am worried it is starting to be noticed. I have a "been there, done that" mentality. Then, just this morning I had an idea: the fact that I am no longer challenged by my job could mean that I am ready for a promotion. I feel that I know everything about this job and, in the three years I have been in it, I have seen everything. Do you think I am ready for a promotion?"

- "Hi, Martin. Thanks for meeting with me today. I will get right to the point. I feel it is time for a promotion. The reason is that I am no longer challenged by what I do. I know I can do so much more, and I want to do more, so please challenge me. Martin, do you agree that I deserve a promotion? If not, what do I need to improve so that I may learn what I need to know right away and be ready then for a promotion?"

■ "Hi Jack. Thanks for meeting with me today. You know I take my job seriously and there is nothing that I would not do for you. I don't know if you have noticed any change recently, but I have to tell you that lately I have been bored. I have been through two complete yearly business cycles, and I am not learning anything new. I have a suggestion: how about giving me additional responsibility and a new title to go with it—you know, a promotion? I am not asking for just a new title. I really want to face some new challenges. I know you have so much on your hands. Let me help you, and together we will continue to be part of a larger winning team. What do you say?"

As an Act of Desperation When There Is No Money for an Increase

■ "Thanks for meeting with me, Larry. I have been thinking about the conversation we had during my annual review. Correct me if I am wrong, but I walked away from that meeting thinking that you were very pleased with my performance this past year. I also felt you were also very frustrated with the organization because it bothered you to have to tell me that the organization was in no financial position at this time to grant merit increases—even to those who truly deserve them. I have a suggestion that might make you feel better—and me as well. How about, in lieu of an increase, you recommend me for a promotion? If you give me a promotion, I will feel terrific that I have been recognized for my work and I will have the opportunity to take on new responsibilities. I don't expect any increase at this time, and I am even willing to wait for my next annual review in October. If you can afford it, and I deserve it, give me an increase at that time to reflect my promotion."

- "I appreciate the fact, Mary, that with so much on your calendar you have demonstrated a personal interest in me by agreeing to meet today. My request is a simple one. With the tight budget we are all faced with for the year that is about to commence, I understand there is no ability at this time to consider merit increases. I am willing to accept that, but I do wish there were some opportunity for you to demonstrate some good-faith gesture that will indicate the organization's confidence in me. I have a simple suggestion as a way to do so: consider me for a promotion. That gesture will have a win-win effect. The organization will be demonstrating their recognition of great performance. For me, it will be a clear indication that the organization appreciates the work that I do and is hopeful that I will stick around to continue moving up the career ladder."

- "Thanks for meeting with me today, Noel. I know that you are frustrated by the organization's current financial condition to approve salary increases. That freeze looks like it will not be lifted anytime soon. I have a matter that I had been putting off, but perhaps now is a good time to mention it. Since there are no merit increases, perhaps it is the right time to discuss a promotion for me. Don't get me wrong, I am not looking for additional money at this time, although that would be nice and I hope that something will be given when the organization can afford it. What I seek is additional responsibility and the recognition that goes with it. A promotion would mean a lot for me at this time."

Phrases for Terminations, Downsizing, or Quitting

Severance packages can include a bundle of terms ranging from salary continuance (annuity payments, lump-sum payouts) to outplacement assistance, COBRA coverage, and other benefits.

Phrases for Quitting That Leave the Door Open

- "I understand that there are no opportunities to increase my compensation (or for promotion or transfer). Even though I have enjoyed my time here, I feel that I owe it to myself to look for positions outside the company. Of course, I would hope that if circumstances change, you would consider me for other positions."
- "To allow myself the time to a devoted job search, I feel that it is in our best interests for me to give a month's notice at this time. This will allow you to find a replacement that I will be willing to train."
- "As you and I have discussed on several occasions, I am ready to take the plunge and start my own company. I am ready to leave immediately at this time but tell me what works best for you."

Phrases for Being Downsized or Terminated

- "The economy has really hit our industry hard, and I do understand the effect it has had on reducing staff in my division. Could I continue part time, retaining some benefits, until I am able to secure another position elsewhere?

- "To avoid being terminated, may I tender my resignation at this time?"
- "May I ask what information the company will share when you are contacted as a reference?"
- "Under the circumstances, I understand the action you feel you must take. In view of my years of otherwise exemplary service, can I ask that you will continue to give me a positive reference?"

Phrases for Severance Negotiation

For an Overview Discussion

- "Thanks for the package, it certainly seems fair. My concern, however, is that I remain whole. Please share with me what you have done for others who have been let go."[2]
- "I appreciate what you all are doing for me. I need to share, however, that it seems what you are offering here is not quite up to what you had provided to others in the past. I would like you to give me the same consideration. It seems only fair that you would do your best to be consistent with the approach that you take and the package elements that you provide."
- "I am, quite frankly, really hopeful that you will be able to do more for me than what we have already discussed. You are aware of my situation, and your suggestion that it will be easy for me to find another job and rebound anytime

---

[2] This approach is good only if you are unable to get information elsewhere. The potential problem is that if they have been stingy in the past, even if they were prepared to offer you a better package than what they had done previously, your question allows them to give you what they normally had done.

soon is not realistic; it's really going to be a tough challenge for me. That said, I really hope you could do something more. Here is what I feel is just and will make me whole as I work toward my next position."

Severance Pay

- "Let me understand the salary continuation portion of the severance agreement. You are offering me one week for each year of service. That will put me in a very precarious financial bind, since the research I have been conducting indicates it will take me at least six months to find a new job."
- "I am concerned that six weeks' pay is less than what others at my level have been granted by the firm in years past. I ask you to please continue to be fair in your severance policies and just provide the same number of weeks pay as you have been doing most recently."
- "It is not the easiest job market out there for people in my profession. It is my understanding that this organization has tried to be fair in the past and really gave severance as a "safety net" so that there would be financial security to bridge the gap from the time this job has been eliminated to that time when another job would be found. I am worried that the weeks' pay that you have mentioned will not get me through this really tough time. I just appeal to you to make me whole when it comes to my pay and benefits."

Setting a Departure Date

- "I know you would like me to leave today. But I do not wish to leave you in a difficult situation, so let me stay until two weeks from now, and I will be sure that this matter is resolved."

- "I realize that none of us is indispensable, but your suggestion that today be my last does not seem practical from your point of view. Let me explain. Not only will you have a vacancy in this position but the day is rapidly approaching when I was expected to participate in the sales meeting scheduled to take place on October 15, with one of our largest prospects."

- "Instead of leaving today, perhaps it would be more practical to let me stay on for a bit longer. Since no one has yet been selected to replace me, you will find yourself in the precarious position in which there will be no one internally who will be able to train my replacement once a candidate is selected, if I am no longer here."

- "I know you would like me to leave today, but why the rush? Why now? If you review my past performance evaluations, you will see that I have been performing well throughout my employment—in both previous positions as well as in the job that I currently occupy. I agree that, if you have determined that my services are no longer needed, I will leave without an argument, but professionally I want to be sure that you are not compromised with my departure. I suggest a reasonable date be selected based on when it is best for the organization. With that in mind, the most effective date seems to me to be March 15."

- "Instead of leaving today as you suggested, let me ask you to allow me to stay until January 20. My reasons are as follows . . ."

Asking for a Letter of Reference

- "Thanks for the severance package. I noticed that there is no mention of a reference letter. Could we include that term, and would you be willing to write one for me whenever the situation requires it?"
- "We haven't discussed letters of reference. May I ask what your thinking is about what to me is a very important aspect of my job search?"
- "As part of the severance agreement I would like to see the draft of the letter of reference that you will send upon request from me. Here is my suggested wording:

  I am pleased to write this letter of reference for John Smith. He had been a key member of the organization since he joined us in 2003. He was an instrumental leader in our strategic change initiatives that addressed state-of-the-art thinking in our complicated industry. Due to environmental conditions that had a severe impact on our revenues, we have been forced to make major restructuring decisions, and John's position was involved.

  You need to know that the termination of his employment is solely due to the major changes in marketing conditions that we have to face today. It is really unfortunate that we were unable to support John's strategic initiatives at this time. If we had, I am convinced that we as an organization would be better positioned to face the future. We just don't have the resources to make that happen and keep him on board.

  If you decide to hire him, regardless of the position, John will quickly demonstrate the value he brings to any job he decides to accept. Your organization will be truly lucky to have him.

  Please call me if you wish additional information regarding his performance."

Staying on as a Consultant

- "Let me suggest a win-win solution going forward. I understand you wish to eliminate this position, and I have no quarrel with that. I do know that there is some unfinished business here that will not take very long to complete. Here is my proposal. You retain me on a consulting basis for two months, so that I may continue to be of assistance, and take the time to ensure that all the work performed here will be moved with consideration elsewhere. I believe that that time span is reasonable. If the work winds down sooner, then the consulting arrangement could terminate at that time."

- "I understand your concern for being able to pay me going forward, and that is why we are having this conversation. Let me propose, for the good of the business, that you "wind down" the position in a reasonable manner. Say in the course of the next 12 weeks, you retain me as a consultant to be of service wherever you need me, so that the position is covered by someone who knows what the situation is, as well as what the customers expect. You save money, since I am no longer employed and you just pay me as a consultant for the time I provide service."

- "Have you considered retaining me as a consultant? I am confident it would be cost effective for you to do so. Here is how it would work. Instead of paying me full time as an employee with benefits, you pay me on a 1099."[3]

Outplacement Assistance

- "Thanks for your offer of outplacement assistance. May I make one request regarding this matter? I know you all have been quite pleased for years with the outplacement firm Job

---

[3] This refers to Internal Revenue Service Form 1099, which is the instrument used to report earnings of independent contractors. The employer needs to be careful that this is a legal use of an independent contractor who had been a former employee. The advice of legal counsel is highly recommended.

Placement Now and the services it has provided. That said, I really would prefer that you allow me to go to Job Placement Now for its outplacement assistance program."[4]

- "Thanks for your offer to pay me an additional $5,000 if I opt out of using the outplacement assistance services that you so kindly provide. However, I know that this is a difficult job market, and I will need all the assistance I can get as I try to find my next job. In fact, I would like you to extend the outplacement assistance from three to six months, because in this job market, positions in my field are few and far between."

- "May I ask that you confirm with the outplacement firm that I be granted the full program and not just the two-day workshop? I know you have done it for others and a two-day program is not going to be really helpful in what I'm afraid may be an extensive job search."

Benefit Coverage (or Extended COBRA Coverage)

- "I understand that I will continue to receive group health insurance through COBRA.[5] When does this benefit start?"

---

[4] Consider carefully your request to select an outplacement firm of your own choosing, because once you do so, you are really, in one very big sense, their client and not the organization's (even though they will pay the bill), since if it were not for you, the outplacement firm would not have your business.

[5] As mentioned in Part Three, COBRA is the acronym taken from the Consolidated Omnibus Budget Reconciliation Act of 1986. One of its provisions is that if employees already covered for group health insurance lose their job for any reason other than gross misconduct, their employer must allow them to continue to participate, for between 18 to 36 months, depending on the situation, in the organization's group health insurance plan, under COBRA. Employees must be willing to pay the entire monthly premium, even though the employer is paying some portion of the premium for all active employees. The employer is permitted to charge an additional administrative fee of up to an amount of 2 percent of the premium to cover its overhead costs for this program. Most employers charge the full 102 percent.

- "I understand that I will have the option to continue to receive health benefits for my family and myself under COBRA, after the effective date of my termination. Now, I am getting awfully close to 65, so I would be able to go right into Medicare coverage from the group plan but only if you continue to carry me as an active employee until my sixty-fifth birthday, which will take place on April 20."

- "I know I am eligible for COBRA, which will allow me to continue to receive health benefits, identical to the ones my family and I were granted when I became an employee. Now I need to ask you to find a way to allow me to contribute a smaller portion than the law allows, since I can't afford the monthly premiums of $980."[6]

Active Employee Health Insurance Coverage

- "How long will I continue to receive health insurance coverage at the same price I do now? With my unused vacation added in, I believe I am entitled to another three weeks pay. If that is true, would you also extend my current benefits by another month before I need to make a decision regarding COBRA?"

- "Our only child is about to reach the end of her eligibility for coverage due to her upcoming birthday. She has just two months remaining: Would you please allow us to stay on the active employee plan for those two months so that when COBRA starts we will pay a reduced premium due to

---

[6] The law does not allow separate amounts to be allocated based on the ability of individual ex-employees to pay 102 percent of the cost of the monthly premium. On the other hand, it is good strategy to raise this issue so that the employer knows that the ex-employee is going to be financially challenged by the prospect of obtaining all the health insurance coverage she is entitled to. It never hurts to ask.

the fact the coverage will only be for my spouse and me? At that time we will no longer require "family" coverage, and that will make a big difference in the monthly premium charges under COBRA."

- "There is one item we have not discussed: health insurance coverage. In an effort to save as much cash as we can from this situation, would it be possible for me to be carried on the payroll for an additional three months so that I can delay determining where the money is going to come from for continuing our health insurance plan here?"

Pension Retirement Vesting

- "Give me recognition for all my time in service by making me whole for retirement purposes by keeping me on payroll until my normal retirement date which is only until May 6."
- "Do you realize that I just had two months until I was fully vested in the pension plan? I need to ask you to please keep me whole and let me walk away with a pension."
- "There are some who are saying that the decision to downsize now was just to keep you from having to meet your pension funding obligations. I don't believe that is true, but I do know that you would be clearing the air if you agree to allow folks, myself included, to stay on the payroll just a little longer so that we may receive what we have already earned and been promised."

Tuition Refund Payments

- "There is one more item that I wish you would consider: my tuition refund. Since I am already in the middle of a semester, can you please continue to pay my tuition refund expenses for the courses in which I am currently enrolled?"

- "Since I only have three courses to go, please allow me to finish my college program with tuition reimbursement for the course of study that I chose and you supported fully until now."

- "As I recall, for the tuition refund program to pay for any employee's schooling, the employee is expected to stay a year after the program has been completed. My idea is simple: due to the restructuring that has been executed, those of us who will lose our jobs have not been afforded the opportunity to freely decide to stay or go. Since that right has been taken away when our jobs were eliminated, we ask you to keep us whole and live up to the payment obligations that you had incurred with employees' already-approved tuition refund courses."

E-Mail Access

- "I have one small favor to ask. Please don't turn off my company e-mail account. Let me continue to use it so that I won't need the additional burden of selecting another e-mail provider as I commence my job search."

- "I know that the policy here has been that when employees leave this organization, their e-mail accounts are shut down immediately. Since these layoffs have been owner induced, let me suggest that for this one time an exception be made to allow those who are losing their jobs to shut down their e-mail files in an orderly manner."

- "Let me suggest that you keep my e-mail account open temporarily so that my customers may continue to have the access you want them to have to key players in our own company. For my part, I will check it daily and refer all the e-mails to the persons you designate to assume these accounts after the restructuring has been completed."

Retention of Office Equipment and Services

- "I know it has been done before, so I am hoping that you will consider my request to keep my cell phone [or PDA, Blackberry, laptop]. I have become so accustomed to it that even though it is not so new anymore, it will really be helpful to me."
- "There is one last item I would like to discuss: the laptop [or any other item]. Would you allow me to keep it? I know it is a bit old, but it is so important to me I would be willing to pay something for it, if need be."
- "One item we have not discussed is the DSL line that you have provided for my use with my home workstation. It would be really helpful if you allow me to use it for just a little longer (say, one month) before it is turned off, so that I may ease the transition of turning over the files to the person taking responsibility for this work."

Continued Voice Mail Access for an Extended Period (For Example, Six Months)

- "We haven't discussed voice mail access. To ease the transition as well as to demonstrate to the marketplace that I have not been released due to poor performance, it will be really helpful if you allow me access to my voice mail for an extended time period. I do think that six months should do it."
- "It would be really helpful to me—and no cost to you—if you allow me to continue to have access to my voice mail for just six months. As I go through the search process, a point of contact here will be one more indication of the terms under which we parted."

- "For an effective transition to occur once I am no longer here on a daily basis, let me suggest that you continue to provide me with voice mail access. I promise to monitor it regularly and to refer any business to the appropriate persons here."

Copying Personal Files

- "As you know I considered my job here a 24/7 one. Since I spent so much personal time working, there is, needless to say, some personal material on my desktop. I ask your permission to let me download it so that I don't lose it before you cut off my access."
- "I have one more small request. I would really appreciate it if you would allow me some time to copy any personal material I may have on my desktop PC."
- "This notice, as you know, came without any prior warning. With that in mind, please allow me access to my computer for a brief time today so that I may be certain that I am not losing any personal data."

If Asked to Sign Additional Agreements [For Example, Noncompete, Nondisclosure (Confidentiality), and No Solicitation][7]

- "I have no problem signing these agreements. Before I do, I have one request . . ."
- "If you wish me to sign these agreements, in exchange, I am hoping you will allow me to . . ."

---

[7] Check the local and state laws first. In some instances, California, for example, the employer needs to offer something in exchange (for instance a severance payment) for your approval on any of these agreements, if done after the original employment agreement (that is, when you were hired).

- "In reading over these agreements, I notice that there is not always an end date. I have no difficulty signing any of them, but I really would prefer to include an end date, since this may interfere with my ability to earn a living."

Part Five

Perfect Phrases for Special Circumstances

If You Have Been Working Per Diem

If you have been working per diem as a temp, substitute teacher, or consultant *and* the position you are applying for specifically asks for your per diem rate, then supply it using the same phrases you would use if asked for your annual salary. If you have been reimbursed for expenses separately, be sure to include that item separately.

- "In my current assignment, my per diem rate is $300 per day, plus travel and living expenses."
- "I am currently earning $300 per day. The income is reported on a 1099 at the end of the year. Since I receive no benefits or travel expenses, I need to pay for both out of my own pocket. Those expenses, of course, reduce my take-home rate."
- "My per diem rates vary from assignment to assignment. The recent range has been $250 to $400 per day. It has depended on the industry (health care, entertainment, financial services), nature of the organization (private versus not for profit), and scope of the project. I also use travel distance and estimated expense in trying to "gross up" the rate. I always also need to pay for my own benefits, under a separate and individual arrangement."

If the per diem rate is a good one then it is to your advantage to share it on that basis for two reasons: first, it demonstrates the pay level you are able to command in the per diem marketplace (one that rewards talent on a very competitive basis); second, that rate may be a premium over what you seek or desire as a "regular" employee (therefore, the potential employer does not get to know what pay level you seek for a full- or even part-time job).

If You Have Been Working on Project-Based Freelance Independent Contractor Assignments

In cases where you have been working as an independent contractor, we suggest you use either a monthly or annualized pay total to make it easier for the reader of your materials to do the math. Be careful, though, if benefits were not part of the pricing. If you want to ensure that you are not at too lofty a level (you don't want to be ruled out of consideration), be sure to also mention that you worked "without benefits," or that "benefits consideration were always my responsibility." By doing so you are demonstrating your reasonableness and reminding the potential employer that even though the rate may appear high that there are other considerations.

In our experience, if you have been compensated for a project on a per diem basis, your rate of pay will most probably be higher than if you were offered a regular employment opportunity. The reason for this is not only due to the absence of benefits, but to the fact that the employer wants to be reasonably sure that you will complete the project before considering other opportunities.

- "Although, due to the nature of my assignments, I have usually been paid on a project basis, converting that rate to a monthly frequency, my most recent rate of pay has been $5,000 per month."

- "Although I was paid on a per diem basis, to help you adjust to a pay rate, based on a 20-day work month, the monthly total is $6,000, or $72,000 per year. The cost of health and retirement benefits has to be factored in, since they were not provided by my client, so I had to pay for the premiums myself. If I were to be offered a position here, as an employee, I would be sure to include the difference in benefit premium expense in any offer that you extend to me."

- My rate of pay is a bit complicated to calculate. In addition to the per diem rate and the absence of benefits, I was also paid a $5,000 bonus at the end of the project for completing the project on time.

If you feel your most recent rate was low, you may mention that fact as well.

- "Although this rate is below the market for the level of responsibility in this assignment, I chose to accept it since it was a not-for-profit organization."

- "Even though the pay rate was below my normal rate of pay, I agreed to do the work as a favor to the organization."

- "Since it was a tough market in which to find work, I accepted the assignment with what I thought was the best price I could get at that time."

Special Phrases for Sales Professionals (or Others with Salary Plus Commissions)

Sales professionals are usually the most direct about their rate of pay. There may be a combination of base pay and commission, draw and commission, and straight commission.

The advantage that sales professionals have is that the person screening their résumés and pay history will, as a rule, be very savvy. The disadvantage is that the sales pro can assume that any statement she or he makes will be subject to the greatest scrutiny. Always be ready to provide proof if requested, such as a pay stub, copy of your most recently completed IRS 1040, or income tax return.

- "My 2006 cash compensation was $75,000 which included my commission and incentive bonus."
- "In 2006, my latest full year, I earned $80,000 for my sales efforts."
- "For all of 2006 I project that my total earnings from commissions and bonuses will exceed $1 million."

Special Phrases for Wait Staff (or Any Other Position Where Most of Your Earnings Come in Tips)

For waiters, waitresses, and all others who depend on tips for the major portion of their earnings, you need to indicate what the appropriate pay level is (and where it came from), to demonstrate improved performance.

- "In 2006, my hourly rate started at $3.25, and after several steady increases it reached $6.15, which was where it was when I submitted my resignation. At the same time, my tips went from an average of $3 to $18 per hour."

- "For the past three years, my total pay, including wages and tips, has increased from $25,000 per year to an anticipated $30,000 for this current year, with wages totaling just 40 percent of that."

- "To give you an estimate of this year's earnings, let me tell you that for the first quarter, my total take-home pay was 40 percent more than the same quarter for the year before—and this is usually our slowest quarter. If recent past years continue to provide identical quarter-to-quarter comparisons, my total earnings for this year will exceed $40,000."

Being Paid "Off the Books" or Being "Grossed Up"[1]

Consider the term "gross-up" here. Gross-up is a calculation that is frequently done for the highest levels of management and expatriate employees. The goal is to make the person whole. Say, for example, that an employee has an overseas assignment that will result in tax consequences, or a hefty capital gains score that will result in an unduly heavy tax burden. In both instances the employer frequently expresses an offer to make the tax payment so that the company absorbs the tax bill (or a portion of it) and not the employee.

---

[1] If you are an employee, it is illegal to be paid in cash, without any taxes taken from your pay. Not only is your employer breaking the law, but you are also a victim of a crime since your employer by his or her action is depriving you of statutory benefits including Social Security, unemployment insurance, and worker's compensation. To report this situation, go to the U.S. Department of Labor Web site www.dol.gov.

Now let's consider the "off-the-books" employee. If the employee were paid $10 per hour off the books, the employee would have no payroll taxes deducted, so the total pay that he or she would receive would be $10 for each hour worked. If the person were paid legally, in addition to the $10 per hour, the employer would have to pay its portion of Social Security along with other payroll taxes that vary from state to state. Consider this breakdown:

Base pay	$10.00 per hour
Social Security (employer portion)	.745
Social Security (employee portion)	.745
Federal tax	2.00
State/local tax	.50
Total Earnings Needed	$13.99

Put another way, for the employee to take home pay of $10 an hour, he or she would have to be paid total earnings of $13.99 per hour, or $559.60 for a 40-hour week, versus $400 (a difference of almost 40 percent) if she or he is paid "off the books." You can see why this illegal method of payment might be attractive to some employers.

For off the books:

- "Will I be paid on or off the books?"
- I would really prefer to be paid on the books, is that possible?"

- "Thanks for the offer but if you do not plan to pay me with deductions taken for Social Security and Worker's Compensation, I will not accept your job offer."

For grossed-up situations:

- "Since I will be expected to pay taxes in both countries, will the organization agree to help offset those consequences by compensating me for the extra tax burden I incur?"
- "Thanks for sharing with me the additional benefits I will be eligible for by accepting this overseas assignment. What accommodation will be made for the additional taxes I will have to pay in total to both countries?"
- "This overseas post sounds like an exciting opportunity and I am inclined to accept but in performing my research I have learned that I will be required to file tax returns in both countries and that, to me, sounds like a nightmare. Will you make a tax advisor available to me as part of the arrangement as well?"

Phrases to Use If a Past Employer Invites You Back

- "Thanks for the phone call and for thinking of me. I would very much like to meet with you to discuss this further. But let me ask, before we do, what do you have in mind?"
- "I understand that this is not the same position as the one I had when I left. Let's meet to discuss this further. Do you have a job description that I could review, so that I come to our meeting prepared? Has a salary range been determined?"
- "Thanks so much for the call. Is this a job offer?"

(If the answer is yes) "Who will the incumbent report to? What is the salary range for the position?"

(Regardless of the answer) "When could we meet to discuss this exciting opportunity in more detail?"

- "I appreciate the call. Please share with me the details."
- "This sounds like quite an opportunity. Am I the only one under consideration?"

(If the answer is yes) "Is this an offer?"

(If the answer again is yes) "What are you thinking of paying for this job?"

(If an amount is mentioned, regardless the level of your attraction) "How soon do you need an answer?"

(Then) "When could we meet to discuss this in more detail?"

Appendix A

Determining Your Current Level of Compensation and "Total Pay" Package

Understanding How Compensation Works

Without requiring you to become a compensation expert, you really need to have a basic understanding of where your current salary level is before engaging in a discussion of pay increases. In organizations with more than 500 employees, there are usually three elements that combine to reflect your current pay.

The first is the grade. A grade is the level where your job is included in the organization's hierarchy. Simply put, when you get a promotion, it is from one grade to the next (when you move from accounting manager to comptroller, for instance, you may move from grade 3 to 4). There may be 10 or more different levels in the organization.[1]

The second element to the pay rate is the range.[2] That is the "spread" that the organization allows its managers to pay for the job. The bottom of the range (the minimum) is the lowest amount the pay system allows, and the highest (the term used is "ceiling") is the maximum.

The last element reflects the point at which your pay is located in the range. Here, in addition to the minimum and maximum of the range for your job you should also be aware of the

---

[1] Banding is the term that is used to build "super-grades." When organizations do so, they combine grades, so that there are fewer of them. The argument for banding is that, in administrative terms, it is easier to execute. We, the authors, don't really think so.

[2] In union contracts, while there are usually no ranges (to eliminate subjectivity from pay levels), there still will be job grades.

following two terms, midpoint and third quartile. The midpoint of the range is the amount the person performing the job at a competent level should be earning. It is usually roughly equivalent to the market price if the organization wanted to go outside and find a replacement without having to train them. In an attempt to be cost effective, organizations may stop granting annual increases to those who have hit that level and may put them on an 18- or 24-month salary review schedule instead.

The third quartile[3] is the pay level beyond which the incumbent may no longer be granted merit pay increases (until the range is raised), unless his or her performance is truly outstanding (or whatever the equivalent is for the highest-performing employees).

The Criteria for Some Salary Increases

So now you understand how your job is pegged when compared to the other jobs throughout the organization. But there is one last element to consider when you are trying to understand how your increase (or lack of one) is determined.

That remaining element to consider is the salary budget. The salary budget is the tool used to let managers know how much in the aggregate they have to award pay increases. Lately, the budget has been generally around 2 to 3.5 percent, slightly less than the inflation rate. The manager therefore needs to determine how to best apportion the funds allotted so that she or he gives the biggest increases to the ones who deserve it the most. Note also that with the small budget, if some get more than 3 percent, others will have to get less.

---

[3] The reason for what many may consider an odd term is due to the fact that each pay range is divided into quarters, and this designation signifies the top of the third quarter.

Below is an example of a grid that managers may be given that shows the boundaries that they must remain within when they make determinations of salary increases. Remember, as much as they are free to do what they wish (as long as they stay within the boundaries shown below), they also need to ensure that the total of their recommendations does not exceed the salary budget allotted. That is the real challenge.

Position in Range of Job Grade Level				
Performance Level	**First Quartile**	**Second Quartile**	**Third Quartile**	**Fourth Quartile**
Below standard	0–2%	0–2%	0%	0%
Meets standard	2–5%	0–3%	0%	0%
Above standard	5–7%	4–6%	2–4%	0%
Outstanding	8–10%	5–7%	5–7%	5–8%

How to Determine Your "Total Pay" Package

Determining Hourly Rates of Pay or Annual Salary

To calculate your annualized salary, take your hourly rate of pay and multiply it by the scheduled hours you are normally expected to work per week. If you are salaried, divide your annual pay by your scheduled hours to determine your hourly rate of pay.

For example, if you are earning $15 per hour and working a 40-hour week, your annualized total will be:

$$\$15 \text{ per hour} \times 40 \text{ hours} = \$600 \text{ per week} \times 52 \text{ weeks}$$
$$\text{per year} = \$31,000 \text{ per year.}$$

Alternatively, if your annual salary is $33,800, your salary is $650 per week ($33,800 divided by 52 weeks per year), and if you work a scheduled 35 hours per week, your hourly rate is $18.57 per hour ($650 divided by 35 hours).

Thinking in Terms of Total Compensation

Reorient yourself to consider not only the tangible rewards for employment but also the intangible rewards. How important is having a prestigious title or corner office to you? Do you need or want a personal parking space? Are flexible working hours or being able to telecommute from home some days a month desirable? Are you indifferent to their stock option plans?

What Is Included in Compensation?

- **Your actual salary and how you are paid.** These usually top the list. Ways to be paid are monthly, semi-monthly, bi-weekly, weekly; commission, or straight salary. Do you like a direct deposit of your paycheck; is it hard to get to the bank?
- **Review period.** Will you be eligible for a review in three months, six months, a year? What are the criteria on which you will be judged, and are they stated or subjective? Who will review you? What hurdles are there to getting an increase if you "pass" review? What is the average increase?
- **Bonuses.** Are they a regular part of the package? What percentage or range is historically given and what performance determines payment—individual or departmental goals? How are they paid; cash or profit-sharing plans? When would you be eligible? What determines who gets bonuses? Who makes the determination?

- **Health, dental, vision, and drug insurance.** Medical protection may be a very expensive proposition, especially if you need to pay for it on your own. It is very expensive for your employer as well. More expensive plans for family coverage sometimes total more than $10,000 per year. Consider the coverage that you currently have, and compare that with what you are being offered where you are planning to move. Make sure that you are making "apples-to-apples" comparisons by looking at the benefits offered as part of a total compensation (or "total pay") package. (For more on total compensation packages, refer to Part Three and review the sections on the topics of negotiating a sign-on bonus and other forms of bonus, options, reimbursement for tuition, conferences/workshops, membership in professional organizations, subscriptions for magazines and journals, child care, health benefits, and time off.) Be sure to include the portion of the premium amount that the employer expects the employees to contribute from their pay. Timing is another aspect to consider in your first-year total pay calculation: how long does a new employee have to wait before coverage commences? What will you need to do to be sure that you have adequate coverage in the interim? What will that cost you? Should you ask your new employer for some consideration here?

- **Work schedule.** From industry to industry, work schedules differ widely. Is the schedule flexible or "set"? Is overtime anticipated? Expected? Paid? What is the policy for sick days, personal days, holiday scheduling?

- **Employee discounts.** Do employees receive discounts for products or services? For some companies, this can be an attractive incentive and can range from being able to get steep discounts on their products to reciprocal arrangements with others for discounts on travel or entertainment.

- **Profit-sharing plans.** Does the company offer a profit-sharing plan? If so, when would you be eligible? What are criteria for payment as well as history of payouts?
- **Perks.** These can be anything from providing a liberal expense account for client entertainment to a special reserved parking spot in the corporate lot. An elite corner office with a view or a fancy title can provide prestige, which is a necessity to doing business in some industries.
- **Tuition refund.** If you are continuing your education in the evenings or on weekends, this can be a substantial benefit.
- **Relocation expenses.** Do you have to move to another location? If so, will the employer pay all or part of your relocation expenses? Is there assistance in finding a new home, or perhaps a mortgage lender?
- **Child care / day care.** Is there a facility on site? Have you been able to visit it? What are the terms of using it: ages of child, payments for use, "sick" child care?

Use the following compensation worksheet to work out your current total compensation. This can be used to ensure that all compensable aspects of your current employment arrangement have been taken into consideration, as well as to compare your current compensation with what you are seeking. Further, two columns have been added to allow you to evaluate job offers you have received. Keep these records for future negotiations.

Total Compensation Comparison Worksheet

Compensation Category	Current	Desired	Job Offer #1	Job Offer #2
Base Salary				
Annual Bonus				
Sign-on Bonus				
Profit Sharing				
Review Period				
Benefits				
Health Care				
Vacation				
Child Care				
Transportation				
Perks				
Title				
Office				
				➡

Expense Account				
Company Car				
Intangibles				
Work Schedule				
Commutation (Time)				
Location/ Environment				
Corporate Culture				

Appendix B

Sample Letters for Wrapping Up Negotiations

Below is an offer letter that is used in an organization of approximately 13,000 employees. If you read carefully, you should be able to identify at least 10 items that are not included and that may be subject to negotiation, if Carol decides that it is worthwhile to pursue them. Refer to the end of this appendix to compare your answers to those of the authors.

Offer Letter

November 24, 2006

Carol Smith
2975 Fifth Ave.
New York, NY 10063

Dear Carol:

This letter is to confirm our offer of employment as Manager, Marketing/Advertising of our organization, where you will report to Vice President Lucretia Murphy. Your biweekly salary will be $3,846.15 ($100,000.00 annualized), and your employment will commence on **December 3, 2006**. Please be aware that this letter is not a contract and should not be construed as one.

This offer is contingent upon your completion of satisfactory results of a reference and background check. Please contact our office to discuss the details of several

➡

mandatory appointments that will be arranged on your behalf. Also enclosed is paperwork needed to ensure that you are appropriately processed for payroll. Please complete these forms and bring all paperwork on your first day of employment, along with all supporting documentation. In order to complete the paperwork process, we will need to see documentation that confirms your eligibility to work in the United States.

Your position makes you subject to a three-month introductory period. Enclosed is a departmental orientation checklist that you will complete with the assistance of your supervisor and return to me.

Carol, I would like to welcome you and trust that this will be a mutually beneficial relationship. We are delighted to have you and I encourage you to contact me at (212) 555–5648 if you need further assistance.

Sincerely,

Justin Ruth
Human Resources Business Partner

The following letters are examples of what you should write to address various situations at the end of the selection process. Your courtesy and determination in taking the trouble to write these in the appropriate circumstances will position you in a more favorable light for future contact.

Thank-You and Acceptance Letter

Date

Name
Title
Company
Address

Dear Ms/Mr/Mrs/Dr _____ ,
Thank you for the time spent with me on _____
(date) and the very informative tour of the facilities. I particularly appreciated the visit to _____ Department and meeting _____ , the Division Head.

   With great enthusiasm I accept the job offer to join your organization as _____ (job title) with an annual salary of $_____. I understand the standard benefit package will include _____ and I will be eligible for salary review in _____ months.

   On _____ (date) I will report to Human Resources at _____ (time) to complete the required paperwork and will start work on _____ (date) at _____ (location).

   Again, I am appreciative of this opportunity to join the _____ team and look forward to quickly making a positive contribution.

Sincerely,

Your Name

Confirmation Letter (If the Job Offer is Not Given In Writing)

Date

Name
Title
Company
Address

Dear Ms/Mr/Mrs/Dr _____ ,

Thanks so much for the offer of employment you extended to me yesterday.

Below is a summary of my understanding.

You have offered me the position of _____ and I will be reporting to _____ (Name/Title). My start date is _____, and, as you requested, I will report to _____ at _____ on that date.

In addition to an annual base pay of $_____, I understand that I will also be entitled to an annual performance bonus of up to _____ but it will not commence until January 1st of my second year. In consideration of that delayed opportunity for additional compensation, I appreciate the $_____ up-front bonus that you are providing in its place.

I also understand from my meeting with the Human Resources Benefits team that my health and dental benefits will commence on _____. Thanks too for agreeing to pay the COBRA premiums from my first day of employment to bridge the gap in coverage.

➡

Per your request, attached is the list of professional references

In closing, let me thank you personally for your assistance in taking the process to a very pleasant and effective conclusion. I am really looking forward to working with you and the other employees at _____. If further information is needed, please contact me.

Sincerely,

Your Name

Declination and Thank-You Letter

Date

Name
Title
Company
Address

Dear Ms/Mr/Mrs/Dr _____ ,

Thank you for the time spent with me on _____ (date) and the very informative tour of the facilities. I particularly appreciated the visit to _____ Department and meeting _____, the Division Head.

After much thought and consideration, although I do appreciate the exciting job offer, I do not feel that my career is heading in this direction at this time.

Or

I greatly appreciate the time and consideration you gave to my candidacy and am disappointed that we were unable to come to mutually agreeable terms. I wish you continued success and, if the situation changes, would be glad to be considered for a different (or comparable) position.

Sincerely,

Your Name

Thank-You Letter (No Job Offer Received)

Date

Name
Title
Company
Address

Dear Ms/Mr/Mrs/Dr _____ ,
Thank you for the time spent with me on _____ (date) and the very informative tour of the facilities. I particularly appreciated the visit to _____ Department and meeting _____, the Division Head.

   Although I felt that my _____ skills and experience with _____ were a match for the position of _____ , I understand that there is great competition to work at _____ (company). Should another position open up that you feel would be a better fit with my skill set, I would be glad to discuss it further with you.

   I wish you continued success.

Sincerely,

Your Name

Authors' Answer Key

Offer letter opportunities for additional negotiation:

1. Sign-on bonus?

2. Other bonuses?

3. Is start date firm?

4. When do benefits commence?

5. Vacation eligibility?

6. Hours (total per week and start/stop times)?

7. Days (five or four?/ Weekends?)?

8. Increase consideration at the end of the introductory period?

9. When will be the first opportunity for increase consideration after the introductory period?

10. Is parking available and free?

Appendix C

Resources

Web Sites

CareerJournal.com; www.careerjournal.com
> Owned by the *Wall Street Journal*, this Web site is loaded with all sorts of job and salary data, including survey information.

Job-Interview.net; www.job-interview.net
> This Web site answers any job interview questions, including those relating to negotiations and compensation, that viewers may pose. The authors of this book are featured and frequent responders at this Web site.

JobStar Central; http://jobstar.org/index.php
> This Web site provides free salary survey data.

PayScale; http://payscale.com
> This Web site provides free salary survey data.

Salary.com; http://salary.com/home/layoutscripts/homl_display.asp
> This Web site is currently the leader in providing free salary survey data.

U.S. Department of Labor; http://dol.gov/dol/topic/statistics/wageearnings.htm
> This is the Web site for the Department of Labor of the federal government of the United States. The department features voluminous and carefully researched data and the results of salary surveys locally, regionally, and

nationally. In addition, the site provides cost-of-living data for various locations throughout the country. The only two negatives are that it sometimes takes effort to find what you are looking for and, because of the careful compilation of compensation research, the pay data, when finally compiled, may be out of date.

Suggested Readings

Chapman, Jack, *Negotiating Your Salary: How to Make $1000 a Minute*, Second Revised Edition, Berkeley, CA, Ten Speed Press, 2001.

DeLuca, Matthew J., *Best Answers to the 201 Most Frequently Asked Interview Questions,* New York, McGraw-Hill; 1996.

DeLuca, Matthew J., and Nanette F. Deluca, *More Best Answers to the 201 Most Frequently Asked Interview Questions*, New York, McGraw-Hill, 2001.

—*24 Hours to the Perfect Interview : Quick Steps for Planning, Organizing, and Preparing for the Interview that Gets the Job*, New York, McGraw-Hill, 2004.

Fisher, Roger, William L. Ury, Bruce Patton (Editor), *Getting to Yes: Negotiating Agreement Without Giving In*, Second Edition, New York, Penguin, 1991.

Kador, John, *201 Best Questions to Ask on Your Interview*, New York, McGraw-Hill, 2002.

Martin, Carol, *Perfect Phrases for the Perfect Interview: Hundreds of Ready-to-Use Phrases That Succinctly Demonstrate Your Skills, Your Experience, and Your Value in Any Interview Situation*, New York, McGraw-Hill, 2005.

Resources

Miller, Lee E., *Get More Money on Your Next Job: 25 Proven Strategies for Getting More Money, Better Benefits, and Greater Job Security*, New York, McGraw-Hill, 1997.

Ury, William, *Getting Past No: Negotiating Your Way from Confrontation to Cooperation*, Revised Edition, New York, Bantam, 1993.

About the Authors

Matthew and Nanette DeLuca are the authors of the best-sellers *Best Answers to the 201 Most Frequently Asked Interview Questions* and *More Best Answers to the 201 Most Frequently Asked Interview Questions*. Matthew is a principal in the Management Resource Group—a human resource consulting, training, and recruiting company. More of their great career advice can be found at www.job-interview.net. Matthew and Nanette are also the authors of *24 Hours to the Perfect Interview* and *Get a Job in 30 Days or Less*.

PERFECT PHRASES
for...

MANAGERS

Perfect Phrases for Managers and Supervisors
By Meryl Runion

Perfect Phrases for Setting Performance Goals
By Douglas Max and Robert Bacal

Perfect Phrases for Performance Reviews
By Douglas Max and Robert Bacal

Perfect Phrases for Motivating and Rewarding Employees
By Harriet Diamond and Linda Eve Diamond

Perfect Phrases for Documenting Employee Performance Problems
By Anne Bruce

Perfect Phrases for Business Proposals and Business Plans
By Don Debelak

Perfect Phrases for Customer Service
By Douglas Max and Robert Bacal

Perfect Phrases for Executive Presentations
By Alan M. Perlman

Perfect Phrases for Business Letters
By Ken O'Quinn

Perfect Phrases for the Sales Call
By Bill Brooks

YOUR CAREER

Perfect Phrases for the Perfect Interview
By Carole Martin

Perfect Phrases for Resumes
By Michael Betrus

Perfect Phrases for Negotiating Salary & Job Offers
By Matthew DeLuca and Nanette DeLuca

Perfect Phrases for Cover Letters
By Michael Betrus

Learn more. Do more.